D0371852

a Carol for Christmas

Other Books by Robin Lee Hatcher

Loving Libby
Catching Katie

The Coming to America Series

Dear Lady
Patterns of Love
In His Arms
Promised to Me

a Carol for Christmas

Robin Lee
HATCHER

bestselling author of *Catching Katie*

ZONDERVAN®

GRAND RAPIDS, MICHIGAN 49530 USA

ZONDERVAN.COM/
AUTHORTRACKER

ZONDERVAN®

A *Carol for Christmas*
Copyright © 2006 by RobinSong, Inc.

Requests for information should be addressed to:
Zondervan, *Grand Rapids, Michigan 49530*

Library of Congress Cataloging-in-Publication Data

Hatcher, Robin Lee.
    A Carol for Christmas / Robin Lee Hatcher.
       p. cm.
     ISBN-10: 0-310-25776-X
     ISBN-13: 978-0-310-25776-9
     1. Christmas stories. I. Title.
PS3558.A73574C36 2006
813'.54—dc22
                             2006010195

Interior design by Michelle Espinoza

Printed in the United States of America

06 07 08 09 10 11 12 • 15 14 13 12 11 10 9 8 7 6 5 4 3 2 1

To Michaelyn and Jennifer,
for so many treasured Christmas memories.
I love you.

a Carol for
Christmas

Prologue

Carol Burke would never forget the day Jonathan drove over her heart. At least, that's what it felt like.

It was the first of September, their eight-month wedding anniversary, and Jonathan had taken the afternoon off from work—a rare occurrence—to spend it with Carol. The day was warm, the sky cloudless, perfect weather for a picnic in the park.

"Hey, babe." Jonathan lifted the wicker basket with his left hand and Carol's guitar case with his right. "Can you get the blanket?"

"Sure, Johnny. I'll get it."

He headed out the door of their small basement apartment, calling over his shoulder, "Better grab the Instamatic too. We might want to take some pictures."

"Okay."

Carol felt happy enough to burst. As much as she loved Jonathan, the past months hadn't been easy—leaving college halfway through her freshman year, adjusting to married life, moving to Boise where she didn't know a soul, feeling a bit homesick and out of place in her new family and her new church. The hardest part, however, had been the long hours, six days a week, that her husband spent at Burke Department Stores. Days like today, when they could spend time together—just the two of them—were too few and far between.

She opened the drawer of the nightstand where they kept the camera. Before slipping the strap over her wrist, she checked the back to make sure there was enough film left in the cartridge. Then she picked up the blanket and headed for the door.

The telephone started to ring.

Don't answer, her heart whispered.

Jonathan stepped into the living room, shrugging his shoulders as his gaze met Carol's. "I forgot the car keys."

The phone continued to ring.

"I'll get it," Jonathan said.

Carol watched as he walked into the kitchen and picked up the receiver.

"Hello? Hi, Dad ... No, I didn't see it ... No ... Well, yes, but can it wait until morning? Carol and I were just ... No ... But—"

Carol hugged the blanket closer to her chest.

"All right. I'll be there in about fifteen minutes. I'll have to change my clothes ... Sure ... Fine. Bye."

Disappointment welled in her chest, although she did her best to stuff it down.

After hanging up the phone, Jonathan turned to face her. "I've got to go back to the store."

"Now?" This wasn't the first time something like this had happened.

"I'm sorry, babe. I'll hurry as fast as I can. There'll still be time to go to the park when I get back."

Carol believed Jonathan meant what he said. But she also knew how determined he was to prove himself at Burke's. It wasn't easy being Arlen Burke's son and, at twenty years old, the youngest manager in the family business. He had to work twice as hard as anyone else to earn the same amount of respect. He would stay at the department store as long as it took to solve whatever the problem was.

"I'd better get changed." Jonathan headed for the bedroom. "I can't go into the store wearing Bermuda shorts. Dad would freak out."

She didn't know whether to cry or to scream. Maybe she should try both. Couldn't they have one afternoon without the store interfering? Is this what it would always be like, Burke's coming before everything else? Was Jonathan going to become a workaholic like his father, the very thing he'd vowed never to be when they began dating?

She wanted to tell Jonathan how she felt, but how could she? She knew he loved her. He was trying his best to be a good provider and a good husband. How could she fault him for wanting to succeed?

Jonathan came out of the bedroom wearing a white dress shirt, a red tie, and a pair of black trousers. When he reached her, he took hold of her upper arms and looked down, his hazel eyes solemn. "I really am sorry, Carol."

"I know."

"I promise to hurry."

"Okay." Once again swallowing her hurt feelings, she walked with him out the door.

At the top of the steps, he stopped to kiss her before striding down the walk to his Ford Fairlane, a high school graduation gift from his parents. As he pulled open the driver's side door, he gave her a quick wave. "Back soon."

She returned the wave.

A moment later, with Jonathan behind the wheel, the car's engine roared to life. Carol saw him wave again, then he looked behind him as he started to back the Fairlane into the alley. A loud crunching sound reached her ears, and the car stopped moving.

She frowned. What on earth?

The car door opened and Jonathan got out. A few steps carried him to the back of the Fairlane. When he turned his gaze in her direction, she somehow knew what had made that horrible sound.

"Carol …"

She hurried forward, but before she reached him, he bent down and lifted the crushed guitar case.

"Babe, I'm sorry."

Not her guitar. Not her most precious possession. Not the friend that had been with her as a teenager on the family farm in Ohio, with her in the dorm as a music student at the University of Colorado, and finally with her in their basement apartment in Boise.

Jonathan held the case toward her, a helpless expression on his face. "I forgot I leaned it against the bumper when I went back inside for the keys."

Tears blinded her as she took the case from his hands.

"Maybe we can get it fixed."

She knew without opening the case that he was mistaken.

"I'll look at it as soon as I get back. We'll get it fixed."

He was leaving? He was going to the store despite what just happened?

"I'm sorry, Carol."

Then he left, and her heart felt as crushed as the guitar.

Chapter 1

Twelve Weeks Later

Homesickness swept through Carol as she listened to Bing Crosby crooning, "I'll be home for Christmas" on the stereo in the living room. Tears of self-pity pooled in her eyes. She missed her parents and younger brothers. She missed her mom's holiday cooking. She missed the farm and her family's Christmas traditions.

"Grow up," she muttered as she rinsed the dishcloth under the running tap water. "You're acting like a baby. Johnny has to work today, like lots of other people."

With a sigh, she looked out the apartment's kitchen window. It wasn't yet 6:00 p.m., and darkness already filled the window well.

"Don't fix dinner for me," Jonathan had said on his way out the door that morning. "It'll be extra late before I'm home."

Carol would have enjoyed going Christmas shopping with Jonathan on this day after Thanksgiving. Of course, even if he weren't working today, there was little money to spend on gifts. They had to count every penny from the salary he made as a junior manager.

Wait to get married, his dad had told them. *Wait until you both graduate from college.*

But they'd been too in love to heed the advice. Higher education couldn't compare with being together for the rest of their lives.

Or so they'd thought.

After draping the dishcloth over the faucet to dry, Carol walked from the kitchen into the living room. A dark-brown secondhand sofa and chair sat against the opposite wall, positioned for the best view of the television set that had belonged to her parents. Four months ago, she and Jonathan had sat together on the sofa—his arm around her shoulders, a bowl of popcorn in her lap—and watched Neil Armstrong walk on the moon.

When was the last time they'd cuddled on the couch while watching TV? They seemed to have so little time together. It grew worse with every passing week.

Another wave of loneliness and homesickness swept over Carol as she sank into the chair. Once again she longed for her guitar, which used to be her comfort in hours like these. Now she didn't even have that.

For as many years as she remembered, her family had spent the day after Thanksgiving putting up Christmas decorations. A fresh-cut evergreen centered before the living room window. Ornaments Carol and her brothers had made at school. Bright strings of lights. Loads of tinsel. A red-and-white tree skirt her mom had crocheted. Hot chocolate and fresh-baked cookies. Turkey sandwiches, leftover dressing, mashed potatoes with gravy. Christmas music playing on the stereo.

"Carol, I'll be working," Jonathan had said when she mentioned decorating the apartment today. "It's the biggest shopping day of the year. Go ahead and do whatever you want about the decorations, as long as we can afford it."

Today she resented her father-in-law and his store more than she thought possible. Arlen Burke was a hard man who expected too much of his only child. If Jonathan had graduated from college with a business degree, he could have joined the family business as a junior partner. Disobeying his father's wishes had cost him that—along with a more substantial salary. Now he was obsessed with proving himself worthy of what he'd lost.

The jangle of the telephone sent Carol hurrying to the kitchen to answer it. Maybe it was Jonathan. Maybe he was on his way home earlier than expected. Maybe they could still go get a tree and put up some lights.

"Hello?"

"Hello, Carol." Her mother-in-law's voice came across the wire. "I wasn't sure you'd be at home."

"Hi, Ruth. Yes, I'm home." A twinge of anger caused her jaw to clench. *Where else would I be? Not with Johnny, that's for sure. He's too busy at the store.* She forced pleasantness into her voice. "Johnny and I both enjoyed spending Thanksgiving with you and Arlen. Everything was delicious."

"And we loved having you. The holiday is meant to be spent with family or it doesn't feel quite right."

Carol thought of her parents and brothers, and her homesickness worsened.

"I just got off the phone with Margaret Osgood, my friend from church," Ruth continued. "You've met her, I'm sure. Anyway, she's looking for volunteers to help with a benefit performance to raise money for the local home for unwed mothers. Travis Thompson is flying in to sing at the event."

Surprise made her forget her homesickness for the moment. "Travis Thompson? *The* Travis Thompson?"

"Do you know who he is?"

"Ruth, he's only one of the top country western recording artists alive." She shifted the receiver from right ear to left as she settled onto the kitchen stool. "Of course I know who he is."

Her mother-in-law laughed softly. "Well, I didn't until a short while ago. I'm not familiar with modern music. I favor old hymns and Mozart. But Margaret said Mr. Thompson will be quite a draw. She also said he's a wonderful Christian who gives generously of his time for events such as ours. He grew up in Idaho. Did you know that?"

"No, I didn't."

"Well, he did. He was raised on a farm near Payette. That's over near the Oregon border." Ruth cleared her throat. "Anyway, would you mind volunteering for the event? I know how much you love music, and it would help you make a few more friends in town. This season is so busy at the store. Neither one of us will see much of our husbands between now and the New Year."

That truth brought Carol back to the present. She missed Jonathan. She'd thought marriage meant spending *more* time together, not less. She'd thought it meant—

"Are you still there, dear?"

She swallowed a sigh. "Yes, Ruth. I'm here. I'll be glad to help out any way I can."

"Wonderful. I'll get back to you with more particulars as soon as I have them. Probably in a day or two."

"Okay."

"Have a good evening, Carol."

"Thanks. You too. See you Sunday." She placed the receiver in its cradle.

Travis Thompson, performing in Boise. Imagine if she got to meet him. She hummed a few bars of one of his hit songs.

Music was like oxygen to Carol. Essential for life. She never felt more alive than when she sang. Once she'd dreamed of having a career as a singer and songwriter, but when all was said and done, she decided she wanted Jonathan more than she wanted a career.

But was the same true for her husband? Did he want her more than that store?

✒

"Your salesclerk tells me you don't have any more of this item." The heavyset woman, her forehead beaded with perspiration, cast an angry look at Sandra Smith—the salesclerk who'd paged for manager's assistance—as she jabbed the folded newspaper with her index finger. "Young man, is this Burke's ad or isn't it?"

"Yes, ma'am. It's our ad." Jonathan strained to keep his voice even and polite.

"Then the management should have planned to have enough stock for your customers."

Jonathan looked at Sandra. "Did you check the back room?"

"Yes, Mr. Burke. I sold the last one more than an hour ago."

He nodded as his gaze returned to the customer. "I'm terribly sorry for the inconvenience. We'd be delighted to give you a rain check."

The woman harrumphed. "As if I would come back to your store." With a toss of her head, she spun and marched away.

"I'm sorry, Mr. Burke," Sandra whispered, tears in her voice.

"It's okay. It's been a long day. Everybody's tempers are getting short." He glanced at his watch. "Only another hour to go."

She gave him a quivery smile as she brushed her cheeks with her fingertips. "It won't come soon enough for me."

"Me either." He patted her shoulder. "Hang in there."

She answered with a sigh and a nod before turning to help another customer.

Jonathan headed for the escalator. The number of shoppers had thinned out over the last two hours, and he hoped to attend to the paperwork on his desk without another interruption. He'd like to get home before ten o'clock.

A few minutes later, he closed the door to his small office on the third floor and sank into his chair. As usual, his gaze moved first to the silver-framed photograph on his desk. Carol smiled back at him, a sparkle in her brown eyes, her curly auburn hair piled high on her head beneath the white bridal veil. He could almost hear her whisper, "I love you, Johnny."

He smiled to himself. Carol was the only person who got away with calling him Johnny. He'd never cared for the nickname. But when Carol said it, it sounded right.

Guilt pricked him, stealing the smile from his lips as he remembered his wife's unhappy, unsparkling eyes when he'd kissed her good-bye this morning. He didn't want her to be sad. But she ought to understand why he couldn't be home, today of all days. Still, he should be more understanding. After all, she was far from her family in Ohio, and the holidays were upon them.

The holidays.

He rubbed his temples, trying to smooth away the pounding in his head. The holidays meant work for the men in the Burke family. When he was a boy, he rarely saw his grandfather or dad during the month of December. They practically lived at the department store throughout the Christmas season.

And now he'd become one of them, leaving early, coming home late, six days out of seven.

Young and stupid. That's what his dad had called him over a year ago when Jonathan announced he was getting married on New Year's Day.

"Is she pregnant?" Arlen Burke had demanded.

Jonathan had responded slowly, controlling his anger. "No, Dad. She's not pregnant. Carol isn't that kind of girl."

"Then there's no need to hurry. Wait until you graduate. You're kids. Son, you're not yet twenty and she's only eighteen. You've got your whole lives ahead of you."

"We don't want to wait. We love each other."

"You've known her less than four months. You can't possibly know that you love her."

"I *do* love her."

"Son, if you leave college, your chances of getting drafted go up. Do you want to find yourself in Vietnam marching through rice paddies?"

"No, but don't you remember what it's like to be in love, Dad?"

"Don't get smart with me."

"Sorry."

"You marry that girl now, and I won't pay another red cent of your college tuition or your rent. You can say good-bye to that business-management degree you were after, and you won't start out at Burke's as a partner either. You'll have to work your way up through the ranks."

"Maybe I don't want a partnership at Burke's. I can get a job right here in Colorado."

Famous last words.

Finding a job in Boulder, where he and Carol met on the university campus, hadn't been as easy as Jonathan thought it would be. Eventually, he'd done the only thing he could—he brought his bride to Boise and went to work for his dad.

Jonathan looked at Carol's photograph again. Would he change things if he had to do it over again? Would he have asked her to wait another two-and-a-half years before they married?

He smiled ruefully. No. No, he wouldn't. Being her husband made everything else worthwhile.

Chapter 2

*C*arol stood on the sidewalk outside the music store, staring at the beautiful acoustic guitar on display in the window. If she closed her eyes, she could almost hear its sweet velvet tone. She would love to touch the mahogany sides, run her fingers over the strings.

Shivering, she drew the fake fur collar of her coat up around her neck and turned from the window. No point wanting what she couldn't have. The price of that guitar was probably as much as Jonathan made in a month. More, maybe. With their current finances, the best she could hope for would be a used instrument from a pawn shop, and even that would be an extravagance.

Head bent into the icy November wind, Carol made her way through the shopping center's parking lot toward the old red-and-white Buick. The bag on her arm held a tree stand, two strings of lights, and a box of tinsel, purchased for the sad little pine tree whose top was poking out of the Buick's trunk.

She jabbed the key into the lock and turned it, jiggled it, then turned it again. Finally, she heard the desired *click* and the lock popped up on the other side of the window. After yanking the door open, she tossed the bag into the car and slid onto the seat, glad to be out of the wind. She was chilled to the bone.

Laughter reached her ears, and she turned to watch as three young couples, walking arm in arm, strolled toward the tree lot. They looked happy, all of them. Whether they were husbands and wives or boyfriends and girlfriends didn't matter. They were picking out Christmas trees together.

A rising envy made Carol sick. True, she wasn't the only wife in the world whose husband had to work on Saturdays. It's just that Jonathan left before nine in the morning, and until the Christmas shopping season was over, she couldn't count on him getting home before nine thirty at night. Usually it was later.

With a sigh, she started the engine, shifted into reverse, and backed out of the parking space. She arrived at the apartment fifteen minutes later to find her mother-in-law's Lincoln waiting at the curb. Rather than driving around to her usual parking space in the alley, Carol stopped the Buick behind Ruth's car.

"I didn't know you were coming over," Carol said as she and Ruth both opened their doors.

"I dropped by on a whim."

Carol grabbed the shopping bag from the seat beside her and got out. "Have you been waiting long?"

"Not long. I hope I'm not intruding."

"Of course not." She stepped toward the older woman and gave her a kiss on the cheek. "I'm always glad to see you."

That was true. While Carol's father-in-law was a brusque sort of man who did not encourage familiarity, Ruth Burke was a woman who exuded joy. Like everyone who knew Ruth, Carol had come to love her.

The two women followed the walk to the back of the house and descended the steps to the apartment. After opening the door, Carol flipped on the nearby lamp before setting her purchases on the floor. "How does some hot chocolate sound?"

"Wonderful." Ruth removed her coat and hung it in the closet. "May I help?"

"No. Just sit and keep me company."

While her mother-in-law settled onto one of the bar stools at the counter, Carol grabbed a milk jug from the refrigerator, poured some into a saucepan on the stove, and turned the burner on low. Then she retrieved the Nestlé cocoa from the cupboard. With relief she saw she had enough for two. It would have embarrassed her no end otherwise.

"This place always makes me think of our first apartment. The kitchen was the size of a postage stamp."

Carol laughed. "This isn't much bigger. I have to keep Johnny out when I'm cooking or we step on each other." A sigh escaped her. "Guess I won't have to worry about him being underfoot for a while."

"It's hard when you're newlyweds. The long store hours, I mean. I know. It was like that for me too."

Carol glanced over her shoulder.

"Has Jonathan ever told you how Burke's got started?"

"A little."

Ruth rested her forearms on the counter. "Arlen was in his early twenties when his father opened Burke Clothing Store. That was in the late thirties, toward the end of the Depression. It wasn't a large store, and at first it wasn't successful. His father didn't have the money to hire other employees. It was a family business, and that meant father and son worked side by side. But Arlen didn't mind because he loved it. Of course, when the war started, he enlisted and was gone more than three years. His father had to carry on alone. But when Arlen got back from Europe, he was bursting with new ideas. That's about the time we met" — Ruth's smile hinted at happy memories — "and it's also when the store started to grow. So here we are, thirty years later, and Burke's has become a statewide chain."

Carol faced the stove again, stirring the milk to keep it from scorching.

After a period of silence, Ruth continued, "I'll never forget the look in Arlen's eyes the day Jonathan was born. He was so excited to have a son to help him make Burke's bigger and better, someone who would take over for him when the time came."

I wonder what Johnny would've wanted if his father didn't have the store. Maybe he would've had big dreams of his own.

Carol poured the chocolate, then carried the mugs to the counter and set one in front of Ruth.

"Carol, Arlen isn't punishing Jonathan for marrying you."

Her eyes widened, surprised by her mother-in-law's comment. She'd never thought Arlen was punishing Jonathan. Oh, she'd known he wasn't happy when they chose to marry so quickly and without finishing college. But she'd never thought ... Or had she? Is that why she resented Jonathan's long days? Because she thought her father-in-law was punishing him — and her?

"Arlen believes everyone must live with the consequences of their decisions. Jonathan chose not to get his business degree. That was his right. But the consequence is that he must learn to run Burke's in a different way. That hasn't changed the fact that his father wants what is best for him." She paused, then added, "And he loves you, dear. Very much."

Outside, the sky grew dark with heavy, low-slung clouds. Snow, the weatherman had predicted. Pondering her mother-in-law's words, Carol turned on another lamp to dispel the gloom in the apartment.

"My goodness. Carol, I nearly forgot the purpose for my visit. It's about the benefit. The committee has worked on the arrangements for some time. In other years, it's been a rather modest affair." She set the mug on the counter. "But once word of Mr. Thompson's involvement got out, we realized this would be much bigger than anything we've done before. We've arranged to use the high school's auditorium so more people can attend. Tickets go on sale Monday."

"I'll help however I can. What is it you need from me?"

"I was hoping you'll be one of the singers. Since the performance is a benefit and will be held so close to Christmas, Mr. Thompson isn't bringing his usual backup group, and he needs us to provide them. He told Margaret that he'd like three female singers."

Carol's heart started thumping. "Me, sing backup for Travis Thompson?" Could she do it? She'd hardly sung a note since leaving college. What if she failed, embarrassing everyone? "I don't know, Ruth."

"My dear girl, you can't possibly refuse. I've heard you sing. And you'll need to help find two other girls to join you. You can hold auditions at the church one evening this week. Mr. Thompson is supposed to arrive on the twelfth, and the benefit is on the evening of Friday the nineteenth. It's not far away now."

"No, it isn't."

"So you'll do it?"

She swallowed hard, excitement replacing fear. "Yes. Yes, I'll do it."

Jonathan could barely see the road four feet in front of his headlights. The falling snow was like a heavy curtain obscuring the world. The Ford Fairlane fishtailed as he turned a corner, reminding him that all four tires were worn thin. He'd have to find the money to replace them soon, especially with snow and ice on the roads.

He eased off the gas pedal, bringing the car under control. A few more blocks, and he would be home.

Exhaustion made his eyelids heavy, and the blizzardlike conditions strained his vision. There was something about headlights on the snow that made him want to close his eyes. Thankfully, he made it home without mishap.

He parked the Fairlane in one half of the detached garage. The owner of the home parked in the other side, which meant Carol's Buick had to remain out in the elements. By now, it must be covered in three or four inches of snow.

After closing the garage door, Jonathan hurried along the sidewalk to the stairwell. He'd shovel the steps first thing in the morning. It was too late—and he was too tired—to do it tonight.

Before he could place the key in the lock, the door opened.

"You're home!" Carol exclaimed, taking his hand and pulling him inside.

"Sorry I'm late again. Dad wanted to go over sales figures after the store closed."

"Johnny, I've got so much to tell you."

He slipped off his coat. Snowflakes dusted the collar and shoulders. He draped it over the back of a folding chair so it could dry outside the closet.

"Your mom came over this afternoon."

"Did she?" He drew his wife into his embrace and kissed her. "Mmm. It's good to be home," he whispered when their lips parted.

"It's good to have you home. I thought you'd never get here."

"I'm looking forward to a day off."

"Me too."

He loosened his hold on her. "The store was nuts all day long. As bad as yesterday. Maybe worse. People pushing and shoving to get to the sale items first. Bah, humbug."

Carol kissed his cheek. "Did you eat supper?"

"Never had time."

"Then come on. I'll heat up something while I tell you what your mom had to say."

Jonathan followed her into the kitchen. "Did she bring more leftovers from Thanksgiving?"

"No, silly. We have plenty. She came about the benefit. Remember, I told you about the fund-raiser last night."

Whatever Carol said to him yesterday was lost in a weary fog. He couldn't remember a thing about a benefit or what it had to do with Carol or his mom. Rather than admit it, he smiled. "Tell me again."

"It's so exciting. You'll never believe it." She opened the refrigerator and pulled out the Tupperware container that held the leftover turkey. Bread, mayonnaise, mustard, and lettuce completed the fixings for his late-night sandwich. "Travis Thompson needs three singers, and your mom asked me to be one of them."

Travis Thompson . . . Travis Thompson . . . Three singers . . . What's Carol talking about?

"When Ruth told me about the benefit, I thought I'd be lucky just to get to meet him." She brought the plate to the counter and set it in front of Jonathan. "And now I've been asked to sing. Can you believe it? I know singing backup isn't any big to-do, but still . . ." She let the sentence drift into silence and chased it with a dreamy sigh.

Carol looked happier than she had in weeks. He didn't want to spoil the moment by admitting he was clueless. He didn't want to confess he hadn't paid attention to what she said to him last night. So he smiled, nodded, and lifted the sandwich with both hands.

"I wish I had a guitar," she added. "I walked by a music store today, and they had a beautiful one on display in the window. If I had a guitar, I could practice more."

Jonathan swallowed hard, guilt twisting his gut. "Maybe next year we can replace it."

"Johnny, I know we can't afford anything like the brand-new one I saw today, but I thought ... I wonder if we could afford something from a pawn shop."

As he put the sandwich back on the plate, he thought of the bald tires on his car plus the payment due on the bank loan for Carol's Buick. And the rent was due on the first. "Our budget's stretched as it is, babe. We'd better wait until spring. I should get a raise by then." The words tasted like failure on his tongue. He'd destroyed her guitar and he couldn't fix it or replace it. What kind of husband was he?

"Okay," Carol replied softly before turning away.

But not before Jonathan saw the disappointment — and disillusionment — in her eyes.

Chapter 3

*I*n the kitchen connected to the church's fellow-ship hall, Carol filled the second of the two large coffeemakers with water before scooping grounds into the brewing basket.

"So, when are you going to make Ruth a grandmother?" Elizabeth Gray asked as she sliced a tray of brownies into tiny squares.

Carol had grown to hate the various versions of that question. "We're not ready yet."

"I'm sorry. I bet you get asked that way too often. We did." Elizabeth glanced sideways at Carol, her left hand resting on her watermelon-sized belly. "That first year we were married, Greg's folks and mine constantly pestered us about grandchildren. Now look at us." She laughed. "Our third child in under four years."

Carol pressed the button on the coffeemaker to start it brewing, then turned toward the other woman. "We want kids. Just not this soon."

After setting the knife in the stainless steel sink, Elizabeth licked chocolate frosting from her fingertips. "When I was in high school, I wanted to become an attorney. I married one instead. Strange, how our lives go off in such different directions from what we planned."

Carol nodded. "That's true. When I was in high school, I wanted to go to Nashville and sing. That was my heart's desire from the time I first learned to play the guitar."

"Really? Wow. I didn't know that about you."

Carol shrugged. "I don't talk about it much."

"Why didn't you go?" Elizabeth awkwardly lowered herself onto a kitchen stool.

"To Nashville?"

"Yes."

"My parents were dead set on all three of their kids going to college. Neither one of them had that opportunity because of the Depression and then the war. My mom's from Colorado and still has family there, so she wanted me to go to the University of Colorado in Boulder. That way, I wouldn't be too far from family if I needed them." She shook her head, remembering how hard it had been for her mother to let her oldest child and only daughter leave home for the first time. "I didn't really care where I went to school as long as they had a college of music. If I had to delay Nashville, I at least wanted to study music."

"And then you met Jonathan Burke."

She nodded, a smile curving her lips. "Yes."

"Love has a way of changing our plans, doesn't it?" Elizabeth stroked her belly again.

"Yes," she answered softly. *But is that a good thing?* She frowned at the thought. *Should I have abandoned my dreams so easily?*

Voices drifted from the hallway into the kitchen, a moment's warning before congregants from the eleven o'clock worship service spilled into the fellowship hall. Elizabeth rose from the stool and carried the brownies to the counter while Carol hurried to get the cream and sugar set out by the coffee cups.

A few minutes later, a squeal that sounded something like her name caused Carol to turn toward the kitchen's side entrance.

"Is it true?" Barbara Matthews, the seventeen-year-old daughter of the pastor, demanded. "Are you looking for singers to perform with Travis Thompson when he's here? That's what Mrs. Burke said. Is it true?"

Carol nodded.

"I can't believe it." Barbara jumped up and down, clapping her hands and squealing her excitement again. "I can't *believe* it. Oh, you've gotta pick me, Carol. You've just *got* to. Travis Thompson is *sooo* cute."

"Is he? I never noticed." Carol forced herself not to smile.

"Are you kidding?" the girl exclaimed. "You've gotta be kidding. He's drop-dead gorgeous!"

The smile crept into the corners of her mouth. "Well, maybe I noticed a little. But I happen to think Johnny is better looking."

"That's 'cause you *have* to think that." Barbara rolled her eyes. "He's your husband."

Carol laughed. "Maybe."

But of course that wasn't why. She remembered as if it were yesterday the first time she saw Jonathan Burke. Almost six feet tall to her five feet one inch, he had broad shoulders, slim hips, and long legs. Nobody looked better in Levi's and boots than he did, then or now. Something about his thick, dark brown hair that brushed his shirt collar had made her want to run her fingers through it. And when he looked at her with those hazel eyes and smiled, she'd immediately thought of a younger version of the Marlboro Man.

Talk about a heartthrob!

"You *will* pick me, won't you?" Barbara's wheedling tone jerked Carol back to the present. "Oh, you've just got to. You've got to."

"No promises. You'll have to try out, like anyone else."

"I've gotta go call Tiffany. She's gonna be absolutely *green*." Barbara spun and disappeared through the doorway.

Carol wondered if she'd been that silly and giddy two years ago when she was in high school. She didn't think so. Full of dreams, yes, but always looking for ways to make them come true, not simply wishing for pie in the sky.

"Be warned," Elizabeth whispered. "She can't sing a lick."

Carol turned around, eyes wide. "She can't?"

"Nope. Like fingernails on a chalkboard."

"Oh, dear."

Elizabeth nodded. "Uh-huh."

More snow had fallen during the morning hours. Jonathan changed his clothes as soon as they arrived home from church and went outside to shovel while Carol fixed lunch.

"Don't forget to bring in the tree," she called to him an instant before the door closed.

The tree ... Snow ... Christmas ... Presents ... Shopping ... The store ... Long hours ... Missing Carol.

At least he got Sundays off, and that was thanks to his mom.

"Arlen," Ruth Burke had said to her husband a few weeks after Jonathan returned to Idaho with his bride, "you can spend twenty-four hours a day in that store if you choose. But your son is a newlywed, and he *will* have Sundays off so he can go to church and spend time with Carol. Do you understand me?"

Jonathan grinned at the memory. His mom was a force to be reckoned with.

He glanced into the nearby window well and caught a glimpse of Carol as she moved around the kitchen. A jumble of emotions turned in his chest.

Jonathan wished he could spend more time with her. He loved Carol more than he thought possible, and nothing made him happier than when he could make her happy. But he felt like he'd failed her a lot lately.

He was doing his best to make sure they had a secure future, and that meant he needed to prove himself to his dad so he could advance at Burke Department Stores. Proving himself to his dad meant he had to work as hard as the old man himself. Harder even.

Finished with shoveling the walk, Jonathan headed toward the Buick. He leaned the handle of the snow shovel against the side of the car, then removed his gloves so he could loosen the twine that tied the trunk down against the treetop.

Carol was right when she said it wasn't much of a tree. But the nicer and bushier the tree, the more those Christmas tree lots charged. This one was within their budget and the right size for their apartment too. Now if he only had something worthwhile to go beneath it come Christmas morning.

He remembered the look on Carol's face when she told him about that guitar at the music store. He remembered her disappointment when he said they couldn't afford one, not even from a pawn shop.

Failure, an ugly voice whispered in his heart. *Loser.*

It was Jonathan's fault Carol didn't have a guitar. First, he'd destroyed the one she had, and now he didn't have the money to replace it.

God, I'm making a mess of things. Help me.

Chapter 4

ord of the tryout for the benefit singers spread quickly, and it wasn't only members of Carol's church who showed up for a shot at singing with Travis Thompson. There were teenagers, women who looked to be in their forties or fifties, and all ages in between. And despite Carol's making it clear they were looking for female singers, there were a few men seated on the folding chairs in the fellowship hall as well. Perhaps they'd come to lend moral support.

I could use a bit of that myself, Carol thought as she climbed the steps onto the stage and walked to the microphone.

Dressed in a navy blue skirt and jacket, she'd swept her auburn hair into a prim chignon, hoping she would look older than nineteen. Nerves tumbled in her stomach. What was Ruth thinking when she asked Carol to be in charge of this?

With her right hand, she lowered the microphone so it was close to her mouth. "Hello, everyone."

The buzz of conversations died.

"My name is Carol Burke, and I'm one of the volunteers helping to put together the December 19 benefit perfor- mance featuring Travis Thompson." She looked at the faces of those in the audience, recognizing the hopes and dreams that were represented there. Hopes and dreams much like her own. "Mr. Thompson has asked us to provide backup singers to perform with him at the benefit. We're looking for only two more female singers." She held up two fingers, emphasizing how slim their chances were.

Glances were exchanged around the room. Some faces registered disappointment, others determination.

"As announced, everyone will be asked to sing portions of the same three songs. I'm sure you'll be familiar with the ones selected. They're popular Christmas carols. All of you who are trying out were given copies of the sheet music and a number when you signed in at the door. Please come up to the stage when your number is called." She turned to look toward the piano on the right side of the stage. Motioning with her hand, she said, "This is Mrs. Atkinson. I've asked her to accompany everyone tonight."

Turning toward the audience again, she saw Ruth standing at the back of the hall. Her mother-in-law smiled and nodded, as if to say Carol was doing a great job. She hoped it was true. She was so nervous her knees almost knocked, not from stage fright but from the responsibility of choosing the other singers. What if she chose someone she shouldn't? Worse, what if she shouldn't even be one of the three?

"Miss Burke," a woman in the front row said, "if we're chosen, what exactly will we be singing? Are these the songs?"

"I'm afraid I don't know. That will be up to Mr. Thompson. I simply selected some familiar carols that I hoped would show your range and ability. Rehearsals will begin on Saturday the thirteenth. If you're chosen, you must commit to daily rehearsals for the full week until the performance. Rehearsal times will depend upon Mr. Thompson's needs and not ours, so it is essential that you be flexible."

She waited to see if anyone would rise and leave the fellowship hall. No one did.

"All right then. Let's have the first person come up here, and we'll get these tryouts started."

Carol hurried across the stage and down the steps.

Please, God. Don't let me blow this. Help me choose the right singers. I'm so nervous, I'm afraid I'll be sick.

Arlen Burke stood on the sidewalk, arms crossed over his chest, staring at the department store's corner window. At long last, he said, "Well, it should draw a crowd. That's for certain."

Relief flooded Jonathan. Coming from his dad, those few words were high praise.

The plans for this Christmas window display had formulated in his mind weeks ago. The life-size, powerful-looking angel and the miniaturized version of sleepy Bethlehem were a definite change from the Santa's workshop, complete with toy train and animated elves, that normally graced this window in December.

His dad turned toward the store entrance. "Your mother and that church bunch will definitely approve of it."

The comment deflated Jonathan's pleasure somewhat. Christmas to Arlen Burke was about store profits, not the birth of Jesus. Financial success was what drove him. He tolerated his wife's and son's faith, but he wanted no part of religion himself. In many ways, the success of Burke Department Stores *was* his religion.

It won't be like that for me, Jonathan promised himself as he followed his dad inside. He had every intention of keeping his priorities straight. He might have to put in long hours right now in order to make his way and provide for his wife, but he didn't plan to lose sight of what mattered most.

The glass revolving door whooshed closed behind Jonathan, and he stopped beside his dad in the aisle leading into the cosmetics department. The air was filled with the scents of expensive perfumes. Jonathan found it overpowering and was thankful Carol had simpler tastes.

He wondered how the tryout was going. He wished he could have been there.

Carol had confessed her nervousness to Jonathan before he left for work. "Why would anybody listen to my opinion? I don't have a music degree or any professional singing experience. Somebody's bound to think I'm too young to be in charge." She released a sigh. "They're probably right."

"That's not true," he answered. "You'll be the most talented person in the room. That qualifies you to be in charge."

Carol gave him a pained but grateful smile before kissing him good-bye.

I should have called her this afternoon. She could've used the encouragement.

He'd meant to call her, but somehow, time got away from him. It seemed like that happened a lot lately.

⟨❧⟩

"Come on," Ruth said. "I'll treat you to a piece of pie à la mode."

Carol leaned back in her chair and closed her eyes. "I'm too tired to eat anything."

Ruth chuckled as she tugged on Carol's upper arm. "I'm not. We'll go in my car and then I'll bring you back to get yours when we're finished."

"All right," she agreed, too tired to resist. Besides, pie sounded pretty good.

It wasn't until they reached the mostly deserted restaurant and were seated in a comfortable booth, menus in hand, that Ruth asked, "So what do you think?"

"Hmm. I'll have the rhubarb."

"Not the pie, Carol. About the tryouts. Did you find two good singers in that group?"

Carol swept loose strands of hair back from her face. "The problem will be narrowing it down to two. There was a lot of talent in that room tonight. I was surprised."

"Yes, but there were more than a few who didn't belong there." Ruth shook her head as she lowered her gaze to the menu. "Some of it was painful to listen to."

Carol recalled Barbara Matthews's singing—a generous word to describe the noise coming out of that pretty throat—and winced. Elizabeth Gray hadn't exaggerated when she said Barbara couldn't sing a lick. And now Carol would have to tell the pastor's daughter that she wouldn't be singing with Travis Thompson.

Ruth patted the back of Carol's hand. "I can read your face like a book, my dear girl. Stop worrying about Barbara. She's young. She'll get over her disappointment."

"I hope so."

"If she can't, she'd better learn quick. Life is strewn with disappointments and heartaches to go along with the good. The experiences we have, good and bad, make us grow into who we're supposed to be. For those who love God, the refining process makes us more Christlike."

Carol felt a sting of conviction. Was she accepting of the things in her life that weren't what she wanted?

The waitress arrived at the table. Carol ordered the rhubarb pie, heated, with ice cream. Ruth chose banana cream pie with extra whipped topping. Both asked for decaffeinated coffee.

"Be right back," the waitress said as she slipped the pencil behind her ear.

Alone again, Carol smiled at her mother-in-law. "I hope someday to be more like you."

"Like me? What do you mean?"

She shrugged. "Peaceful. Accepting. Contented. Joyful." *All the things I'm so often not.*

"Oh, my. Am I all those things?"

"Yes."

"I believe ... No, I *know* such attributes come with maturity, and I hope I have them. But I'm afraid your description makes me feel older than Methuselah."

Carol leaned forward, smiling. "You're not old. And I'm so glad you're my mother-in-law."

"My dear, I'm thankful for that too." Ruth patted Carol's cheek. "God blessed me when Jonathan chose you for his wife."

❧

There was no sign of Carol's Buick when Jonathan pulled into the detached garage shortly after nine thirty. That surprised him. He hadn't figured the tryout would last so long.

Minutes later, he entered the dark apartment, turned on the nearby lamp, then shed his gloves and coat, dropping them onto the chair. Every little sound he made seemed amplified in the silence. He couldn't remember the last time he'd come home from work and not been met by Carol's welcome.

He went into the kitchen and checked the refrigerator for something to eat. He'd had a sandwich at his desk around four. Now he was hungry again. But nothing he saw enticed him, so he settled for a tall glass of milk. After guzzling it down, he returned to the living room, turned on the TV, and sank onto the sofa. Another few minutes and the local evening news would be on. He would watch while he waited for Carol. He grabbed one of the small throw pillows and put it behind his head as he stretched out on the sofa.

Closing his eyes, he remembered again how nervous Carol was that morning. Maybe he should have insisted he leave work early so he could go to the church with her. He'd thought about it, but then his dad wanted to go over some invoices from one of their suppliers. They discovered several discrepancies. Worse, the errors were Jonathan's fault. By the time he straightened things out, it was closing time.

He rubbed his fingertips against his temples. A year ago, when he and Carol were still at the university, they often stayed up late, planning their wedding and dreaming about the life they would share as a married couple. Never once did he imagine they would spend so many hours apart. Never once did he imagine he wouldn't be able to provide for his wife better than this. If only...

Exhaustion overtook him, and he was asleep before the newscast began. In the morning, he wouldn't remember Carol's arrival home or making his way to bed at her encouragement.

Chapter 5

$\mathcal{T}$he next week went by in a blur.

Carol made her choice regarding the other female singers and called everyone about her decision. The benefit committee met twice, once in Ruth's home and once at the high school where the performance would be held.

On Monday of the second week in December, Arlen Burke decided he and his son should visit the other Burke stores in Idaho. The trip would last three days and two nights, as long as the weather cooperated and the roads stayed in good condition.

This was the first time Carol and Jonathan had spent a night apart since their wedding. She missed him. Missed him more than words could say. The loneliness, the emptiness of the apartment, seemed to taunt her, and she wondered, for the first time, if this was the life she wanted.

The thought frightened her.

$\mathcal{Q}$

"I have a surprise for you," Ruth said when Carol answered the telephone Thursday morning. "Two surprises, actually."

"Good ones?" Carol watched snowflakes falling into the window well. Were the roads getting slick? Would

Jonathan still get home tonight as he'd promised, or would she have to spend another night alone?

"Absolutely. First, I've found a guitar for you to use."

Carol straightened in her chair. "Really?"

"Yes. Pearl Iverson's grandson is in the army, and he left his guitar with her. As long as you take good care of it, she said you're welcome to use it."

She would be able to practice, to accompany herself when singing. Surely that would lift her out of the winter doldrums. "What sort of guitar is it, Ruth? Do you know?"

"Heavens, I haven't a clue. But I can bring it to you today and you'll see for yourself."

"I'll take good care of it. I promise. Please tell Mrs. Iverson that."

"Of course. Now for the other surprise. Mr. Thompson is flying into Boise a day earlier than expected. I'm going to pick him up at the airport this afternoon and drive him to his hotel, and I'd like you to come with me. Can you be ready by one?"

"One o'clock?" Nerves erupted in Carol's stomach as she glanced at the clock. "Yes, I can be ready."

"Terrific. I'll pick you up. See you soon."

After returning the phone to its cradle, Carol hurried into the bathroom and checked her appearance in the mirror.

She was about to meet Travis Thompson. He was famous. He'd made gold records. People listened to him on the radio and they bought tickets to hear him perform. He'd achieved everything she used to dream of.

Dreams she'd given up to marry Jonathan.

Did I make a mistake? Did I give up too much, too soon?

She closed her eyes against sudden tears. What was she thinking? She loved Jonathan. Singing was wonderful, but she loved her husband more. She wouldn't want to be without him. Not in a million years.

Would she?

She choked back a sob. Half frustration, half shame.

"Lord," she whispered, eyes still closed. "I'm sorry. I don't mean to be ungrateful. What's wrong with me? How could I even think such a thing?"

She felt a little better when she opened her eyes. Not completely better but a little. That was something.

Black ice coated the surface of the interstate. Strong gusts of wind slammed against the side of the Cadillac every few miles as Jonathan drove west out of Pocatello, headed toward Boise.

While Arlen Burke was careful never to curse in front of his wife, he wasn't as careful in the presence of his son, especially when the Cadillac fishtailed its way across an overpass, bringing the passenger side dangerously close to the guardrail before the rear wheels grabbed pavement again.

"Sorry, Dad."

"Where'd you learn to drive?"

Through clenched jaws, Jonathan answered, "Driver's ed, West Junior High, summer of 1964. Perfect score on the exam."

His dad said nothing for a few moments, then laughed. The rare sound caught Jonathan by surprise.

He remembered when his dad opened the new store in Pocatello. "Expansion," Arlen called it, and his excitement had been palpable, even to a little kid. Jonathan had loved riding with his dad over to Eastern Idaho. He loved tagging along as his dad walked through the store with the manager, going over details, making suggestions for display changes, coordinating upcoming sales.

When did Dad stop laughing? When did he stop having fun?

Jonathan cast a quick sideways glance to his right. His dad stared straight ahead, the smile already gone, leaving his profile as cold as the snowy countryside they passed through.

"Your father's a good man, Jonathan," his mother often said. "Don't judge him too harshly. He has a God-sized hole in his heart, and he's tried to fill it with work, with his achievements, and with money. He hasn't learned yet that only Jesus can fill that hole. We must keep praying for him to find his way to the Savior."

It was hard to believe *that* would ever happen.

If there was one thing Jonathan wished he could change about his life, it was his relationship with his father. He loved his dad and wanted to please him, but he never felt like he measured up to the old man's expectations.

The lengthening silence in the automobile allowed his thoughts to drift, and he recalled Thanksgiving last year. He'd gone with Carol to Ohio to meet her family. How different they were from his own.

Carol's dad owned a dairy farm, and her mom and two younger brothers worked right alongside him. They didn't have a lot, materially speaking, but their home was full of love, laughter, and faith. The whole family liked to play practical jokes, and Jonathan had learned over that long weekend to keep an eye out for mischief of one kind or another.

He felt a sudden longing for his wife. He wanted to tell Carol how much he loved her. He wanted to thank her for being patient with him. He wanted to promise her that he wouldn't let Burke Department Stores run his life.

Carol stood beside Ruth and watched as Travis Thompson—wearing a leather jacket and a black cowboy hat and carrying a guitar case slung over his shoulder—appeared out of the Jetway. In her mind, Carol heard Barbara Matthews squealing, *"Travis Thompson is sooo cute!"* Truer words were never spoken.

"Mr. Thompson?" Ruth raised a hand and waved. "Mr. Thompson, over here."

Tall, lean, rugged, the singer grinned as he strode toward them.

"Mr. Thompson, I'm Mrs. Burke. We spoke on the phone."

"Yes, ma'am. Nice to meet you." He tugged the brim of his hat.

Ruth put an arm around Carol's shoulders. "This is my daughter-in-law, Carol Burke."

"How do?" He repeated the hat tug toward Carol.

"It's a pleasure to meet you, Mr. Thompson." She had to swallow to keep from blurting something stupid like, *I'm such a fan ... I always wanted to be a singer too ... I own all your records.*

"The luggage claim is this way." Ruth motioned with her left hand, then started walking. "My daughter-in-law will be one of your backup singers. She's enormously gifted. You'll see for yourself. Last week she held auditions for the others who will perform with you. Everyone is ready to begin rehearsals when you are."

"I'm looking forward to working with you, Mrs. Burke."

It took Carol a moment to understand he meant her and not Ruth. Color flushed her cheeks. "I'm the one looking forward to it, Mr. Thompson. And please, call me Carol."

"Be glad to, as long as you both call me Travis. I'm not partial to too much formality. 'Specially not when I'm back home in Idaho among my own folks."

Travis had such a friendly, unassuming air about him that Carol could almost believe she walked beside just another Idaho cowboy — if not for the way people stared at them as they followed the concourse toward baggage claim.

The stares made her feel a little famous herself.

She liked the feeling.

He's home!

Carol spun away from the window and raced to the apartment door, flinging it open before Jonathan reached the bottom of the steps. "I'm glad you're back." She hugged him, unmindful of the briefcase he held in one hand and the suitcase in the other.

Jonathan brushed his lips against hers. "Me too. Amazing how much longer that drive takes when the roads are slick."

"Brrr." She pulled him inside and closed the door. "It's freezing out there."

"Yeah." He dropped his bags on the floor, removed his gloves, and unbuttoned his coat. "It was even worse in Pocatello and Idaho Falls. They've got close to a foot of snow on the ground."

Carol had so much to tell Jonathan, but looking at his face and listening to his voice dampened her excitement. He was exhausted. But when wasn't he exhausted these days?

He hung his coat in the closet, then turned and drew her into his embrace. He leaned closer as if to kiss her, but then he stopped, his gaze moving beyond her right shoulder. "What's that?"

She turned to see what he meant. The borrowed guitar. Ruth had given it to her this afternoon.

"Carol, you didn't buy a guitar, did you?"

"No, I—"

"Because I told you we need to wait." Irritation sharpened his voice. "We can't afford it. Not yet."

She took a step back. "I didn't buy it, Johnny. Your—"

"Then where did it come from?"

From the guitar fairy. Where do you think?

He crossed the room and picked up the instrument. "This looks new." He glanced at her again. "Carol, we can't afford this."

Anger flared in her chest, and she imagined herself taking that guitar and smashing it over his head. If the guitar were hers, she might have done just that.

"I'm too tired for this," he said softly, more to himself than to her.

"You're too tired. Too tired to listen? Too tired to believe me?" She stepped forward and grabbed the guitar from his hands. "I didn't *buy* this. It's a loan from a friend of your mother's."

He had the decency to look ashamed, but it didn't cool her temper. She was just getting started.

"If you were home once in a while, you'd know these things. You'd know someone was loaning me a guitar."

"Carol, I—"

"And I wouldn't need to borrow one from a total stranger if you hadn't been so careless with mine."

Surprise widened his eyes, followed immediately by a kind of kicked-dog expression that almost broke her heart. Almost, but not quite. She was too angry to let herself feel anything close to sorrow or regret or sympathy.

"Johnny, all you think about is yourself, your dad, and that stupid store."

"That's not true."

"Yes, it is." She set the guitar on the sofa. "You don't know how awful it is for me, being alone, waiting for you all the time." She marched into the kitchen and pulled the lid off the frying pan where she'd kept his supper warm. "You're not the only one who knows about managing money. I'm not an imbecile who doesn't know better than to spend money we don't have."

"Carol, please."

She whirled to face him. "You know, Johnny, you got the future you were working toward. You went to college so you'd be ready to manage Burke Department Stores. Yeah, by marrying me, maybe you're having to do it a different way, but you're still going to have it." She patted her breast-bone. "What about me? What about my music? There were things I wanted too. And I don't even have my own guitar because you were reckless with it. You just don't care about what I want."

In your anger do not sin, a voice whispered in her heart.

She turned to the stove, tears streaking her cheeks. It wasn't fair, what she'd said. It wasn't true. She knew Jonathan cared.

"I'm sorry, Carol." His hands rested on her shoulders. "I'm really sorry. I never meant to hurt you. Not with your guitar. Not by working all the time."

As suddenly as it had come, her anger dissipated.

He turned her around, and she pressed her cheek against his chest. "I love you, babe." He kissed the top of her head as he drew her tighter to him. "This won't last forever. Honest." With an index finger beneath her chin, he lifted her face toward him. "Honest. It won't last forever." He kissed her, long and slow and loving.

In his arms, with his mouth against hers, Carol forgot not only her anger, but all the news she'd meant to share with him.

Chapter 6

*A*bove the down comforter, the bedroom was cold, but beneath it, spooning with her husband in those few minutes before complete consciousness took over, Carol was warm and content, the worries, frustration, and anger of the previous day forgotten.

Reluctantly, she opened her eyes and looked at the clock radio. It was after seven.

"Don't get up," Jonathan whispered near her ear. "I'll call in sick."

"Your father would never believe you."

"I don't care."

She rolled over to face him, although he was little more than a shadow in the darkness of the room. "That's not true. You care what he thinks. You care a lot. You want him to be proud of you. And you like the idea of building on what your grandfather and father started."

He groaned. "I'm not so sure. Maybe I should've been a banker or a schoolteacher or —"

"It won't last forever," she quoted him. "Proving yourself to your dad won't last forever."

He released a wry laugh. "Seems like it will." He pulled her closer, resting his chin on the top of her head. "This isn't how I imagined things would be when we got married."

Me either.

He kissed her forehead, then rolled onto his back, staring at the ceiling in the dim light of the basement bedroom. "He isn't a bad guy, you know. My dad."

"I know."

"He's just kind of"—he turned his head on the pillow, looking toward her—"absent from the lives of those who love him."

Tears pooled in the corners of her eyes as she reached out and touched his cheek with her fingertips.

"I'm not going to do that to you, Carol. I'm not going to be emotionally absent from you. So help me, I won't."

"I know," she said again, hoping it was true.

"I've gotta get through this holiday shopping season. It wouldn't be right for me to do anything else now. But come January, Dad's going to have to make changes in my schedule or I'll leave Burke's. I'll find another job."

Carol loved him so much in that moment, she thought her heart might burst.

"Will you hang in there with me until then?"

"I'll hang in there with you forever, Johnny Burke. I'm sticking to you like glue."

Jonathan stood on the loading dock, staring into the back of the truck. "These items were supposed to be delivered to our Pocatello store. We're already overstocked here."

"Look, kid." The truck driver, a man in his late forties with two day's growth of beard and greasy-looking hair, wiped his nose on the sleeve of his coat. "I drive where I'm told, and the orders said to bring this truck to Boise. I'm unloading this stuff, whether you like it or not."

"No, sir, you're *not* unloading here. The bill of lading clearly states—"

"What seems to be the trouble?" Arlen Burke strode toward them.

Jonathan hoped his dad hadn't heard the driver calling him a kid. He hated looking ineffective in the old man's eyes.

"Well?"

The driver's entire countenance changed. He became subservient in Arlen's presence. "Seems we've got a mix-up in the orders, Mr. Burke."

"Jonathan," his dad said. "You're wanted on the telephone. I'll take care of this situation. You go and take the call."

He didn't want to let his dad handle it. He wanted to do it. He wanted to make the surly driver think twice before calling him a kid. Okay, so he was half the age of most of the guys on the dock, but he was still a manager.

Yeah, a manager with only one-and-a-half years of college and no degree. The boss's son, who had inherited his position rather than earning it. No wonder nobody took him seriously.

He turned on his heel and walked to the back entrance of the department store, frustrated beyond words. The day had started out so good too.

In his office, he punched the blinking line button and picked up the handset. "This is Jonathan Burke."

"Hi, honey. It's me."

"Carol?"

"I'm sorry to bother you at work. I know you're busy."

"It's okay," he said, even as he thought how much his dad hated employees taking personal calls during business hours.

"Your mother is hosting a get-together tomorrow night to welcome Travis Thompson. She thought it would be nice if he could meet all of the volunteers and the board of directors for the girls' home. Anyway, I want you to be there with me. Do you think you can get away from the store earlier than usual? It starts at seven. I know Ruth will want your father to be there too."

He heard the wistful desire in her voice. After the fight they had last night, the last thing he wanted was to disappoint her again. "Sure, babe. I'll be there." *Somehow.*

Carol smiled as she hung up the telephone. She'd been afraid Jonathan would say he couldn't get off work early, the same way he hadn't taken time off the day after Thanksgiving.

She walked into the living room, and her gaze went first to the sad little tree next to the television. Only it didn't look so sad today. The lights, tinsel, and ornaments had transformed it more than she expected. And hadn't she and Jonathan enjoyed themselves just as much, decorating it together on a Sunday afternoon instead of the Friday after Thanksgiving? Of course they had.

Taking the borrowed guitar in hand, she sank onto the sofa and strummed a few chords.

This morning, after Jonathan left for work, a melody had started running through her mind. At first she thought it must be something she'd heard on the radio, but now she knew it wasn't. It was something new. It was hers. It was a song waiting for lyrics.

She hummed a few bars, then searched for the right combination of chords. Tried. Failed. Tried. Failed. Tried. Succeeded. With the melody, but no lyrics came to mind.

Again, she smiled, but this one was self-deprecating. Songwriting never came easy to her, as much as she loved to do it. Maybe when she saw Travis, she could ask him for pointers.

Chapter 7

The church fellowship hall buzzed with conversation on that Saturday morning, reminding Carol of the night of the tryouts. Only this time, there were fewer people making the same amount of noise: the two women who'd been selected to sing with Carol in the backup group, one alternate singer in case someone got sick, and three members of the Travis Thompson band, who'd arrived late last night in their bus.

Carol had tried on numerous outfits this morning before leaving the apartment. She wanted Travis to look at her and think, *Country singer.* Silly, she supposed, to want anyone to think that when it wasn't true.

"Here he is now." The drummer played a *ba-bum-bum* to emphasize his announcement.

Travis grinned as he strode across the hall, looking every bit the star that he was. "Hey, fellas," he greeted the band. "Glad to see you made it. How were the roads?"

The bass guitarist answered, "Pretty clear most of the way."

"Good." Travis turned toward Carol. "Howdy." He gave the brim of his hat a tug.

"Hello."

"Mrs. Burke's not with us this morning?" he asked after a quick glance around the fellowship hall.

"No. She's at home getting ready for tonight's reception."

"I'm looking forward to that." He turned toward the members of his band. "Let's get started. Fellas, in case you didn't introduce yourselves, this is Carol Burke. Carol, meet Hank, Friday, and Gart. We've been playing together since we were kids. Went to the same schools. If they cause you any trouble, you tell me and I'll knock some sense into them." He turned toward the three other women in the room, a look of expectation on his face.

Carol made quick introductions. Maddy Gladstone was a thirty-five-year-old wife and mother of three who sang in the church choir. Catalin Ibarran was perhaps five years older than Carol, unmarried. She worked as a secretary in the state attorney general's office. The alternate singer was Sara Chandler — thirtyish, divorced, and extraordinarily pretty.

"Glad to meet all of you," Travis said, wearing his trade-mark grin.

Over the next fifteen minutes, while Travis explained his expectations, Carol imagined herself as a permanent part of his band. What must it be like to be on the road, driving from event to event, performing before thousands of fans? She wondered about the backup singers who regularly traveled with him. Were any of those women a love interest? Would any of them eventually make it in Nash-ville and record their own albums?

Carol had loved country music long before *Hee Haw*, Glen Campbell, and Johnny Cash made the style more popular to television viewers. She enjoyed rock 'n' roll, but country owned her musical heart. How wonderful it would be to stand on the stage of the Grand Ole Opry. Wouldn't she love to be present for live performances by Tammy Wynette, Dolly Parton, and Loretta Lynn?

"Carol?"

She blinked, realizing how far her thoughts had wandered, and met Travis's amused gaze.

"Let's have the three of you stand over here"—Travis pointed to a spot to the left of the band—"and we'll give a listen to how you sound as a group."

That was the end of Carol's daydreaming. For the next two hours, she was completely attentive, and she loved every minute.

She could hardly wait to tell Jonathan all about it.

At 6:45 p.m., as Jonathan hurried toward his car, not wanting to be late to his mother's reception, someone discovered a fire in one of the storage rooms off the loading dock. After ordering the evacuation of the store, Jonathan and a few other men managed to recover much of the merchandise before the firemen arrived and forced them to stand out of harm's way to watch and wait.

The fire marshal would later tell Jonathan that the fire was likely started by a cigarette butt carelessly tossed aside. The good news was, they'd avoided a major disaster for the store, its customers, and its employees. Except for a cut on Jonathan's hand, no one was hurt in the incident, and the evacuation of the store had taken place with smooth efficiency.

Carol checked her watch. Almost nine and still no sign of Jonathan. Even her father-in-law was here, mingling with the guests and making idle conversation. Arlen had told Carol that Jonathan was coming right behind him.

He promised he'd be here. He promised.

She looked around her in-laws' living room. A fifteen-foot Christmas tree stood in front of ceiling-to-floor windows that overlooked the lights of Boise. The fresh scent of pine filled the air. Carols played softly in the background. It was a merry party, people talking and laughing. A perfect party ... except her husband was absent.

Again.

Travis Thompson stood on the opposite side of the room, surrounded by guests, both women and men, who listened to him with rapt attention. When his gaze caught Carol's, Travis nodded toward those around him, spoke what must have been an apology, then made his way through the crowd toward her.

"You're looking mighty alone, Miss Carol. Don't care for the party?"

"It isn't that." She glanced at her watch again. "I'm wondering what's happened to my husband. He should have been here two hours ago." She tried to sound more concerned than angry, though it was the latter emotion that gnawed at her stomach.

"Well, while I've got you to myself, there's something I'd like to tell you."

She looked up into his eyes and was reminded of Barbara Matthews's description: drop-dead gorgeous. But if he knew how others saw him, if he knew the effect he had on women, he took no advantage of it. He was always the gentleman.

"You've got a terrific voice, Carol. Have you thought of singing professionally?"

Her heart fluttered. "Yes."

"Country music?" He gave her one of those charmingly crooked grins that appeared on album covers.

"Mmm. I've loved country music since I was a little girl. My parents made a deal that if I graduated from college, then they'd help me financially when I went to Nashville."

"So what happened?"

"I met Johnny, and we fell in love." She shrugged. "Idaho's a long way from Nashville, and my husband's career is here."

Travis nodded and his eyes said, *Heard that before.* "Does your husband realize how talented you are?" He leaned closer. "Do *you* realize it?"

She drew a quick breath through her nose, her eyes widening. *Am I? Am I really?*

"When we rehearse on Monday, I'll bring you my agent's contact information. If you decide to try singing professionally, you can give him a call." He smiled again. "And don't ever think it's too late. Plenty of careers have started decades after musicians got married and had families. You keep that in mind. It's never too late."

It felt too late. Here she was, standing beside a huge country star, a man only about ten years older than she was, a man whose face and voice were known by thousands upon thousands of people. Would she have been in his position ten years from now if she'd chosen differently?

From the corner of her eye, she saw Arlen and Ruth weaving a path through their guests. When she looked in their direction, her mother-in-law made a subtle but definite motion with her head, indicating Carol should join them. She didn't want to follow. She wanted to stay right where she was and let herself pretend that her dreams could still take wing.

But she didn't stay. "Excuse me a moment, Travis." She turned from him and followed her in-laws out of the living room and through the dining room.

Swinging the kitchen door open before her, she opened her mouth to inquire what was wrong. Then she saw Jonathan, leaning against the refrigerator, and the question lodged in her throat. His hair was disheveled. His face and clothes were smudged with what looked like soot, and his left hand, which he held against his chest, was wrapped in gauze.

"How bad is it?" his father asked.

"Not bad. That one storeroom is ruined, but there wasn't much merchandise in it. We got out everything we could.

No real smoke or water damage inside the store itself, just in the storage area. It could've been worse. Much worse."

"No customers injured?"

"No."

"You should have sent for me."

"I took care of it, Dad. That's what I'm there for, isn't it?"

Carol stepped forward, drawing her husband's gaze. "Johnny, what happened?" The anger she'd felt a short time ago had dissipated like mist. "Were you in an accident?"

"There was a fire at the store. It's out. Everything's okay."

A fire? Her heart tripped. "What happened to your hand?"

"I cut it on something. It needed a few stitches. It hurts, but it's nothing serious." He gave her a reassuring smile. "Honest." He looked down at his dirty suit. "But I don't think I'm in any condition to mingle with Mom's guests. Would you mind if I went on home and skipped the party?"

Carol stepped closer. "Are you sure you're all right?"

"I'm sure." He leaned forward and kissed her lightly on the lips. "I'm okay. Just badly in need of a shower. You stay here and have fun, and I'll see you when you get home."

Everything in her wanted to stay. Jonathan was all right. He'd said so himself. Carol wanted to return to stand beside Travis and hear him tell her again that she had the talent to make it as a country singer. She wanted to talk about his agent and ask him questions about Nashville and mention her attempts at songwriting. She wanted to know more about going on the road. She even wanted to know why he'd never married. She wanted to pretend for an evening that things were different.

Guilt washed over her, shame that she thought of her own enjoyment when her husband was hurt. He could have been killed. "No. I'll go with you, Johnny." She turned her head. "Ruth, will you—"

"I'll make your excuses to everyone. You take Jonathan home, in your car. We'll drive his over tomorrow afternoon."

Wordlessly, Carol nodded as she reached to take hold of Jonathan's arm, then walked beside him toward the back entrance of the house. For her, the party was over.

Carol came awake with a jolt, the nightmare lingering at the edges of her consciousness. Fear lingered too. She turned her head on the pillow and listened. Jonathan's breathing was deep and steady.

She slipped from the bed and padded on bare feet to the window, grabbing the down comforter from the foot of the bed as she passed. The air in the bedroom was chilly. Jonathan turned the heat down to sixty at night. It felt more like forty. She wrapped the comforter around her shoulders.

Moving aside the curtain, she saw a sliver of moon —God's thumbnail, she'd heard it called—surrounded by a blanket of stars. The glow of the moon and the stars seemed brighter because of the snow-covered earth below.

Leafless trees stood stock-still, no breeze to stir their branches. Silence reigned throughout the neighborhood.

In her dream, she'd looked for something ... or someone. She was outside on a night much like this one, cold with only the light of the moon to see by. The streets, alleys, and buildings were strange to her. In the odd way of dreams, it was Boise but not Boise at the same time. She ran and ran, up one street, down an alley. Looking, looking, looking but never finding.

"Finding what?" she whispered. "What did I lose?"

Yourself.

Tears slipped down her cheeks.

Help me, God. I'm lost and don't know what to do about it.

Marriage wasn't supposed to be this hard, was it? Shouldn't love make it easy for her to know what was right and what was wrong? How could she love Jonathan and yet yearn for something more? Worse, something else.

I came to Boise with him. I gave up everything to be his wife. Would he go with me to Nashville if I asked him? Does he love me enough to make sacrifices?

Stupid questions. Here in Boise, Jonathan had a future. He would inherit Burke Department Stores from his father. If they went to Nashville, they might starve to death before anyone took notice of her. The music industry was overflowing with girls like her, with talent and big dreams, who never would make it in the business.

But Travis said I could make it in Nashville. God, didn't You want me to use my talent? Why else would You give it to me? Just so it could go to waste? Sure, I can sing in the shower or even in the choir at church, but is that it? If I could be a singer like Travis, if I made record albums and performed at the Grand Ole Opry or on Hee Haw, *then I could do benefit performances to raise money for good causes too. I could do so many good things for You.*

She wiped the tears from her cheeks with the edge of the blanket.

I want more, God. I can't help it. I want more.

Chapter 8

*J*onathan placed his hand on the small of Carol's back as they walked into the church narthex. Ever since he awoke this morning, he'd felt a need to touch her, as if afraid she would suddenly disappear.

His mom, who stood visiting with friends before the start of the service, smiled when she saw them. "Good morning." She joined them near the sanctuary entrance. "How're you feeling, Jonathan?"

"Fine." The truth was, he didn't feel great. His chest felt a bit smoky, and he'd swear there was soot trapped in his eye sockets. One thing he knew for sure: he wasn't cut out to be a fireman.

"Your father wants you to call him at the store as soon as you get home from church. Something about the lost inventory."

A whisper passed through the narthex like a ripple spreading across the surface of a pond. Heads turned toward the hallway that led to the church offices and Sunday school rooms. Curious, Jonathan followed suit.

Carol's hand alighted on his arm. "That's Travis Thompson." She sounded a little breathless.

Jonathan didn't much care for that breathless quality when it was attached to some other guy's name. Particularly when the man in question was handsome, rich, and famous. He watched as the country star strode toward them, Pastor Matthews at his side.

Travis Thompson wore a black suit, a white shirt, and a tie. Not much different from what more than half the men in the congregation wore on any Sunday morning. But other men didn't draw the rapt attention of nearly every female in sight.

Jonathan glanced at Carol. Was she as captivated by this singer as the rest of the women appeared to be?

Jealousy curled in his gut like a venomous snake.

Last night on the drive home from his parents' house, Carol said she had something exciting to tell him. Something Travis had told her. But before she could share what it was, Jonathan started coughing. When he finally caught his breath again, she said she would tell him later. She never had. After Jonathan showered, he'd crawled into bed and fallen asleep almost before his head hit the pillow.

He should have remembered to ask her about it.

She's not happy with me.

He thought back over the weeks since Thanksgiving. No, he'd have to go back further than that. For months he'd spent more and more time at the store, and too often, during what little time he spent with Carol, he'd been thinking about the store.

He recalled the night they'd fought over the borrowed guitar. Sure, they made up. Carol loved him and she'd forgiven him. He didn't doubt that. But that didn't change the fact that he was unable to make her happy the way he wanted to.

"Good morning, Travis," Carol said.

The singer smiled. "Morning."

Carol touched Jonathan's arm. "This is my husband, Jonathan Burke."

"Pleasure to meet you." Travis offered his right hand.

Jonathan shook it. "Pleasure to meet you too." He hoped he sounded sincere.

Travis returned his gaze to Carol. "Your pastor asked if I would start the worship service with a song. I'd like you to join me."

"Me?" she asked, her eyes widening.

Everything in Jonathan wanted to object. Not to Carol singing ... but to Carol singing with Travis Thompson. The reaction made him feel small, petty, and unchristian. He pressed his lips together, swallowing his words of protest.

"What would we sing?" Carol asked.

"'Silent Night.' Like we rehearsed it yesterday, only without the band. Just a guitar. Are you willing?"

She hesitated only a moment before answering, "Yes."

"Guess we'd better get up to the front then." Travis looked at Jonathan. "I'll bring her back when we're done."

Jonathan was tempted to punch the guy right in the schnoz. In the rational part of his brain, he knew Travis meant he would escort Carol back to wherever Jonathan was when the song was finished. But he wasn't thinking with the rational part of his brain. Jealousy — all green, ugly, and pathetic — had taken hold.

Travis offered the crook of his arm to Carol. After a quick glance and smile toward Jonathan, she took it, and the pair walked down the center aisle. By the time the singers reached the altar, Jonathan and his mother had slipped into their usual pew.

Someone Jonathan didn't know—probably one of the band members—brought Travis his guitar, and the celebrity slipped the strap over his head. Then he leaned toward Carol and said something. She nodded. His fingers strummed the guitar strings, and the sanctuary fell silent.

Travis Thompson knew how to work a crowd. He waited a full minute, his eyes downcast, before he played a few chords and then began to sing.

"Silent night, holy night, all is calm, all is bright …"

Carol's voice joined Travis's.

"Round yon virgin mother and child …"

Jonathan supposed those around him were inspired by the beauty of Carol's crystal-clear voice, the notes rising toward the sanctuary rafters. What he felt was fear.

"Holy infant, so tender and mild, sleep in heavenly peace …"

He'd heard Carol sing many times before. But not until this moment had he understood the full nature of the gift God gave her.

Understanding it terrified him.

She could have had more out of life than what Jonathan offered. Lots more.

He wondered if his love was enough to hold her.

Carol closed her eyes and allowed joy to fill her heart as she sang, her voice blending with Travis's. She wasn't nervous, as she thought she might be when he asked her to join him. It helped, of course, that this was one of her favorite Christmas carols. She'd loved singing "Silent Night" since she was a little girl. She knew every note, every word. It also helped that she sang with a pro, a man who'd performed before thousands of people.

"Heavenly hosts sing alleluia; Christ the Savior is born! Christ the Savior is born!"

As the last strains of the song faded, Carol opened her eyes. For a few moments, the sanctuary was dead silent. Suddenly, wonderfully, the congregation began to applaud. Softly at first, then louder and louder.

"Thank you, Carol," Travis said, raising his voice enough for her to hear over the clapping. "That was beautiful." He offered his arm once again.

She took hold, smiling, her ears filled with the continuing applause.

"Is there anything more wonderful," Cal Matthews said from the pulpit, "than voices lifted in praise to our Lord?"

Carol felt a catch in her spirit as Travis escorted her down the steps. Was that what she'd done? Had her voice been lifted in praise? Had she thought of the Lord as she sang the beloved carol? Or had she thought only of herself and the way she sounded to others? Was it joy she'd felt . . . or pride?

Carol was quiet on the drive home from church, and Jonathan didn't have the courage to attempt a conversation. What if she said something he wasn't ready to hear?

She'd looked so beautiful as she sang "Silent Night," her eyes closed, her face tilted upward. Her auburn hair had turned fiery red beneath the lights of the altar area. If he hadn't known better, he would have thought she and Travis had sung together for years.

What she'd wanted—the singing career, the record deals, the fame, all the dreams she'd shared with him when they first met—was within her grasp. Jonathan sensed it, deep in his soul.

Lord, don't let me lose her. Show me what to do. Tell me what to say.

But all he heard in reply was the fearful beating of his own heart.

Chapter 9

*C*arol was exhausted by the time she arrived at the Monday evening rehearsal. But her weariness didn't come from physical exertion. It came from a spiritual wrestling match not yet finished.

There is now no condemnation for those who are in Christ Jesus. Isn't that what the Bible said? Yes. In Romans. She'd read it in her devotions last week. So why did she feel guilty? Why did she feel condemned? What was so wrong with singing?

Nothing. It wasn't singing that was the problem, and she knew it. The problem was her motivation, her secret desire for something she didn't have. In the deepest corner of her heart, she wanted to sing for all the wrong reasons. She wanted fame. She wanted glory. She wanted a life she didn't have now.

Rebellion welled in her heart, stacking bricks of silence between her and Jonathan in a growing wall.

Carol entered the fellowship hall with her thoughts churning. She discovered she was the last to arrive. "I'm sorry." She glanced at her watch. "Am I late?"

Travis waved her forward. "No, you're not late. The rest of us were early."

Carol pulled off her knit cap and stuffed it into her pocket before removing her coat and laying it on a folding chair. When she turned around, she found Travis coming toward her.

He held out his hand, a white card held between his thumb and index finger. "I brought this for you."

"What is it?"

"My agent's business card."

She hesitated, heart fluttering, then took it from him.

"I talked to Ken earlier today and told him you might give him a call. He's hoping you will."

Could this be happening? Was Travis Thompson really telling her to call his talent agent? He'd mentioned it the night of the party, but it seemed too good to be true.

It must be God's will for her to have this information. It must be God's will for her to pursue a singing career in Nashville. Otherwise, why would He cause Travis to give her this business card?

The Bible said that God would give her the desires of her heart as long as she delighted in Him. How could she look upon what was happening as anything other than His will?

Is it, Lord?

"Hey, boss," the drummer called. "Stop chewin' the fat with the pretty lady and let's get to work."

Travis laughed. "Hank's right. We've got lots to do before this Friday's performance."

Carol nodded. She would rather sing than think anyway. Singing was easy. Thinking was giving her a headache.

❧

Jonathan sat at his desk, Carol's photo from their wedding held between his hands. But it wasn't her picture he saw. It was the memory of her standing at the front of the church yesterday.

He'd been selfish. From the day they first met, he'd been selfish. He'd asked her to give up everything for him. He'd known her hopes and dreams, but once they fell in love, he expected her to leave all those things behind. And she had.

What had he given up for her? His college degree? A better-paying entry into the family business? Yes, but neither of those things was permanent.

No, he gave up little when they married. Carol had sacrificed all. For him. If only he could pay her back in some small way. If only he could make her see how much he loved her, how much he needed her, how much he wanted to make her happy.

If only *he* could be enough...

He opened the desk drawer and removed his checkbook, flipping it open to stare at the balance in the register. Not much there. He still needed to buy new tires for the Fairlane, and now there was the telephone bill waiting to be paid too.

Not enough. Not nearly enough.

❧

Two hours later, Carol turned off the lights in the fellowship hall and walked outside with the others, making certain the door to the church was locked behind them. The temperature had fallen well below freezing while they were inside. Carol clutched her arms over her chest as she headed for her car, escorted by Friday Jones, the bass guitarist.

"You and the other gals are doing a great job," Friday said as they walked, his shoulders hunched forward and his hands jammed into the pockets of his jeans. "This is gonna be a good show."

"I hope so."

"You can know so. You're good. Travis doesn't give out the name of his agent to just anybody."

She glanced toward Friday. He was a skinny beanpole of a guy with pale blond hair and piercing blue eyes. "You and Travis have been playing together a long time."

"Yeah. We formed our first band when we were in junior high. Travis could always sing, of course, but as a group, the boys weren't anything to write home about. I never figured we'd be doin' this all these years later or that we'd go the places we've gone."

Carol pulled up the collar of her coat. "Do you like the traveling?"

"Some of it's good. I'm a small-town boy who's seen London and Paris and Rome." He shook his head. "But the road's not easy, that's for sure. It's tough on relationships. Livin' in buses and hotel rooms and all the time spent apart from the people you love. Gart and his wife got divorced last year 'cause she couldn't take it no more. Hank was engaged a couple years back, but they never made it to the altar. His girl found herself a schoolteacher to marry. You know, a fella who comes home by five every night."

They arrived at the Buick, and Friday opened the door for Carol.

"What about you?" She gripped the top of the door as she looked at the guitarist. "No one special in your life?"

He chuckled, his breath clouding before his mouth. "I do have a girl, as a matter of fact. She's a waitress in Nashville. I think we might make it."

"And Travis?"

"Nah. Not for a long time." He shrugged. "Women kinda throw themselves at him, him bein' a performer and rich and good-lookin' to boot. But he's an old-fashioned guy, and his faith runs deep. He doesn't want a gal who's seein' stars. That's made him a bit gun-shy when it comes to women. That's not to say he doesn't want love, marriage, and a family. He does. It's just he figures God'll tell him when the right gal comes along, and he's willin' to wait till He does."

Carol smiled, a sweet memory flowing through her mind. "That's how I felt when I met Johnny. I knew he was the one God meant for me." She gave Friday a little wave and slipped into the car; he closed the door after her. "See you tomorrow night," she called before turning the key in the ignition.

As she drove home, she didn't think about Nashville or the agent's card in her purse or even the upcoming benefit performance. She thought about Jonathan, wondering what her life would be like without him.

She couldn't imagine it.

Would a career in country music fill that place in her heart if he wasn't there? She didn't know that either.

But was it necessary for her to choose between her husband and a career? Couldn't she have both?

Chapter 10

ad." Jonathan stepped into the president's office.

Arlen Burke leaned back in his chair. "What's up?"

"Just wanted you to know I'm leaving now. Tonight's the benefit."

"As if I didn't know. Your mother's talked of nothing else since that singer got to town."

"This is an important night for Carol. It means a lot to her. I think she's nervous." Of course, he didn't know for sure; they'd barely talked all week. And every additional minute of silence seemed to make it harder to speak again. "I want to be with her before the show, lend my support however I can."

"Of course you want to be there. Get going."

Jonathan must have let surprise show on his face.

"I'm a married man myself." There was the hint of a grin in the corners of his dad's mouth as he spoke. "I may not be a sentimental fool, but I love your mother and try to support her in her hobbies and volunteer work."

This is different, Jonathan wanted to say. *This is more than a hobby or volunteer work. She's got amazing talent. She's got a gift. She's so good, it scares me.*

But he didn't say anything. He'd been shackled by the unspoken, trapped by missed opportunities, paralyzed by what-ifs.

"I'll see you at the high school, son."

"Yeah. See you there." Jonathan turned and left.

As he exited the rear door of the department store, he checked his watch. Carol was supposed to be at the high school by five thirty for a short rehearsal before the doors opened at six fifteen. He had almost an hour before he needed to be at the apartment. That gave him plenty of time to stop at the florist shop to buy a bouquet of long-stem red roses.

Hang the budget. He meant to splurge on his wife, tonight of all nights.

Carol stared at her reflection in the bathroom mirror. Her hair was all wrong. She'd tried putting it up. She'd tried leaving it down. Nothing looked right. Her appearance would undoubtedly embarrass Travis, the members of his band, and the other two singers standing with her.

Worse, she probably wouldn't sing the right notes. Or, for that matter, remember the words to any of the songs. She was going to bomb. There was no doubt about it. She would bomb.

Breathe, Carol. Breathe.

She closed her eyes and inhaled through her nose, then let it out through her mouth.

Better? Yes, that was a little better.

She turned from the mirror and her gaze fell upon the new dress hanging against the bathroom door, a gift from Ruth. Black and white sequins glittered beneath the clear-plastic dress bag. A box on the floor in her bedroom held black-satin heels with rhinestone clips on the toes.

At least her clothing would be flawless, even if she flopped in every other respect.

Breathe.

She flipped off the bathroom light and walked to the kitchen, where she poured herself a cup of hot water from the teakettle. Leaning her hip against the counter, she took small sips as she stared out the window.

It was almost dark outside, but at least it wasn't snowing. The sky had remained cloudless all day. Another storm front wasn't forecast to arrive until Sunday. That was good news. It meant the roads would be clear for those coming to the benefit. Last she'd heard, it was expected to be a sold-out performance.

Oh, my. *Breathe.*

She wished Jonathan would get home.

The steering wheel of the Ford Fairlane pulled against Jonathan's hands, and then came the unmistakable *thump*, *thump*, *thump* of a flat tire.

"No. Not now!"

The red roses lay in a box on the seat next to him, but buying those special flowers for his wife took longer than anticipated. Darkness had fallen over the city while he was inside the florist shop. Now he barely had time to get home and change his suit if he was to have Carol to the high school by five thirty.

The car rolled to a stop at the curb. Jonathan got out. Sure enough, the left front tire was flat as a pancake. He should have bought new ones. He'd known this would happen eventually.

He leaned back into the car and yanked the keys from the ignition, then strode to the trunk, aware of each precious moment as it passed.

She wouldn't let herself cry. It would ruin her makeup.

With the shoe box under her right arm and the dress bag slung over her left arm, Carol walked to the Buick. She had five minutes to get to the high school. She never should have waited this long for Jonathan.

Oh, there would be an excuse, a reason for his tardiness. Maybe a good one, maybe a not-so-good one. Maybe another fire on the loading dock. Maybe his father had an inventory list to check. Or maybe he had a customer who couldn't find a lipstick in the right shade.

Him and his father and their stupid department stores.

Why had she left college for this? Why had she thought God wanted her to marry? Maybe that wasn't what God wanted for her. Maybe He hadn't told her Jonathan was the one. And if she'd been mistaken about Jonathan and marriage, did that mean she had to remain in Boise, lonely and unfulfilled, and let go of her dream?

As she hung the dress on the hook in the backseat of her car, Jonathan arrived, pulling the Fairlane into the empty parking space beside her. She didn't look up, didn't want to see him right now.

"Carol, I'm sorry."

She slammed the back door of the Buick.

"Honey, I had a flat tire. Give me a minute to change and I'll—"

"Don't bother. I'm late as it is." She pulled open the driver's door.

"Carol, please. I just gotta wash up. Wait for me."

She looked at him. "I don't have time to wait for you, Johnny. I've got to go now."

"Okay," he acquiesced softly. "But I'll be there soon."

She didn't think she cared, and she didn't bother to reply.

❦

He watched her drive away, her words echoing in his ears.

"I don't have time to wait for you, Johnny. I've got to go now."

He had a sick feeling in his gut that she meant much more than tonight, much more than needing to get to the high school by five thirty.

"I don't have time to wait for you, Johnny. I've got to go now."

He was afraid she didn't have time to wait for him in this lifetime, that she meant to go now, that she meant to go somewhere he couldn't follow.

The final medley of the evening—"The Christmas Song," "Silver Bells," and "White Christmas"—was a duet by Travis and Carol. When the last notes of "White Christmas" faded into silence, the audience erupted in applause and whistles.

"Thank you, Boise!" Travis shouted above the clamor. "Merry Christmas!"

The clapping continued as the members of the band and the other female singers joined Carol and Travis in center stage. They bowed and waved at the audience.

"God bless you!" Travis called. "Good night!"

The curtains pulled closed in front of them.

"Man," Friday said above the continuing noise, "you two blew 'em away. Carol, I never heard anybody sing better. Not even Travis. You've got me in the mood to deck a few halls myself."

She felt an odd mixture of pleasure and disappointment. She'd loved every minute of the performance. Had Jonathan liked it? Was he in the audience? She wished—

"Friday's right," Travis said. "You were the star of the show. Come with me a sec." He took hold of her elbow and gently drew her toward the left wing.

She went with him, the applause filling her ears. It was a heady sound. What would it be like if—

"Carol." Travis stopped walking. "I'd like you to meet my agent, Ken Hill."

Lost in thought, she hadn't noticed the man standing offstage until that moment.

"A pleasure to meet you, Miss Burke." The agent offered his hand.

"And you," she replied, stunned, taking it.

Perhaps in his fifties, Ken Hill wasn't a tall or particularly imposing man, but Carol knew he was a powerful figure in the music business.

"Travis tells me you're interested in country music. I'd like to talk to you about it."

"Carol?"

She turned. Jonathan stood in the shadows of the wing, a beautiful bouquet of roses in his arms. When their gazes met, he stepped forward, holding the flowers toward her.

"You were amazing," he said.

Tears pricked her eyes as she took the roses from him. "Thanks." A cacophony of emotions tumbled inside her. She loved him. She was mad at him. She wanted to be in his arms. She wanted to be anywhere but there.

"Jonathan," Travis interjected, "let me introduce you to Ken Hill. He's my agent. Ken, this is Carol's husband, Jonathan Burke."

Once again, Ken offered his hand. "Mr. Burke, I was just telling your wife I'd like to talk to her about her career."

Something Carol couldn't define flashed across Jonathan's face.

"I'd like to represent her. If she's willing to come to Nashville, I think Carol's got a chance at making it big." Ken looked at her again. "Give me a call after the first of the year."

More people appeared in the wings, pressing in, eager to meet Travis, wanting to shake his hand and get his autograph.

Ken Hill gave Carol a business card identical to the one Travis had given her earlier in the week. "I'm serious," he said, leaning closer so she could hear him. "You call me."

She nodded.

"Nice to meet you, Mr. Burke," Ken said to Jonathan, then he disappeared into the crowd.

Carol might have thought she'd imagined the encounter, if not for the white card in her hand.

Jonathan's worst fears were coming true, right in front of his eyes. He was losing Carol to the music she loved. The music she might even love more than him.

Looking dazed, she turned toward him. "Do you *know* who that was, Johnny?"

"An agent." His tone was clipped.

"Not just *any* agent. He's everybody-who's-anybody-in-country-music's agent." She glanced down at the card. "And he wants to represent me. *Me*, Johnny. He wants me to go to Nashville."

Jonathan felt like a boulder had fallen on his chest. "Are you going to go?"

"How could you ask me that?" She shook her head, a look of disbelief in her eyes. "This is the chance of a lifetime. How could I *not* go?"

He drew a long, deep breath and let it out before answering. "What if I don't want you to go?"

She drew away as if he'd struck her, and he felt like a heel. Worse yet, he didn't know how to take the words back, how to make things better between them again.

He lowered his voice to a near whisper. "Let's talk about it when we get home."

She glanced over her shoulder toward Travis and his fans, then looked at Jonathan again. "Maybe there's nothing left to talk about, Johnny."

With those words hanging in the air, she walked away from him.

Chapter 11

On Christmas Eve, Carol was home alone while Jonathan was at the store dealing with the last-minute shoppers. Not that his absence made much difference. They'd barely spoken to each other in the five days since the benefit. A gray shroud hung over the apartment and the entire holiday season. The future looked even darker and more uncertain.

Carol sank onto the couch, blinded by tears.

"God," she whispered, "I don't know what to do. I'm so unhappy. I can't believe Johnny's acting this way. How could he not want me to go to Nashville? Why can't he see that You gave me the ability to sing and that I should do it? It's the desire of my heart, and You're delivering it into my hands. How could Johnny be so selfish?"

And what about your own selfishness?

"I'm not being selfish. He'll inherit the stores eventually. His life won't change a bit."

The tears slipped from her eyes and streaked her cheeks.

Of course going to Nashville would change his life. It would change both of their lives. For better or worse, it would change them.

"It couldn't get much worse than it is now."

Sniffing, she reached for a tissue and wiped her cheeks, then blew her nose.

"It's unfair," she muttered. *I love him, but I'm so angry with him. He's being unreasonable. I'm in the right here.*

"Would you rather be right or right with God?" her mother would have asked.

Carol leaned her head against the back of the sofa and closed her eyes, wishing she could talk to her mom about this. What would her father tell her to do? What would her mother say if Carol told her everything?

Oh, how she missed their counsel.

At home in Ohio, the family would soon be sitting down to a supper of ham and turkey, mashed potatoes, yams, and all the other fixings. Her brothers would jostle each other and brag about which one could pile the most food on his plate. The house would be filled with the scent of the new pine wreath her dad had hung over the fireplace, as he did every Christmas Eve. Her mother's favorite Christmas albums would be playing on the stereo — Bing Crosby, Mel Tormé, Barbra Streisand, Frank Sinatra.

Despite her sorrowful mood, Carol smiled as she imagined her brothers asking — as usual — if they could open one gift before the family bundled up, got into the car, and drove to church for the Christmas Eve service. And she could hear her mother giving the answer she always gave: "No. You'll have to wait."

Life was simpler back home on the farm. Things rarely changed there.

Opening her eyes, Carol straightened and picked up the agent's card, staring at the black print on its face as she'd done so many times in the five days since the benefit.

What should I do? Oh, God, what should I do?

The phone rang, and she looked toward the kitchen, tempted to ignore the jangling summons. It was probably Jonathan, calling to say he would be late getting home. And what would it matter? The Burkes didn't do anything on Christmas Eve except attend the church's candlelight service, and that wasn't until eleven thirty. They waited until Christmas Day for their dinner and gift giving.

What would she and Jonathan do to fill up the empty hours tonight?

With a sigh, she rose, shoved the business card into her pocket, and went to the kitchen. "Hello?"

"Happy Christmas Eve, darling."

"Mom?"

"We couldn't wait until morning to call you. Are you surprised?"

"Of course."

She pictured her mother, wearing her red-and-green Christmas apron, a bit of flour on her cheek.

"Hey, sis!" her brothers shouted in the background. "Remember. No presents until after church."

Carol laughed as tears pooled in her eyes. "Tell those goofballs I miss them. I miss all of you."

"We miss you too."

"Have you got lots of snow?"

"Indeed we do. The youth group from church took a sleigh ride last weekend. You remember how much fun those are."

"Fun and cold."

"True enough. Before I forget, Ruth called last Sunday and told us how wonderful you were at the concert. I wish we could have heard you."

"Me too." She rested her forehead against the wall next to the phone.

"Your father wants to talk to you now. I love you, darling. Merry Christmas to you and Jonathan and his parents."

"I love you too. Bye, Mom."

A shuffling sound came across the wire as the phone exchanged hands.

"Merry Christmas, Carol."

"Same to you, Dad."

"Your mom's got the place all decorated and a great supper about to go on the table, but it doesn't feel right without you. Wish you and Jonathan could've come to see us this year."

"Me too."

"Did you get the gifts we sent?"

"Yes. The packages are all under the tree."

"Good. Good. Never can tell about the mail service this time of year."

"Did you get ours?"

"Sure did. Wasn't necessary, of course. I know what it's like to be young and broke." He laughed. "Come to think of it, I know what it's like to be older and broke."

"But somehow you always managed, Dad."

"True enough. With God's help, we always have. Jonathan home yet?"

"Not yet."

"Well, you tell him Merry Christmas from all of us."

"I will, Dad." She knew the call was drawing to a close. Long distance was expensive. She should tell him about the agent and Nashville before it was too late. She should ask his advice, quick, while she had the chance.

"We'll say a prayer for you and Jonathan at the church service tonight."

Tears ran down her cheeks. "We'll do the same for all of you."

"We love you, hon."

"Love you too, Dad."

"Boys, say good-bye to your sister."

More shuffling of the phone, followed by a shout. "Bye, sis. Merry Christmas."

"Bye," she whispered. "Merry Christmas."

After she heard the disconnect on the other end, she hung up the telephone, sniffing noisily as she reached for another Kleenex.

It hurt Jonathan to see Carol cry. She missed her family a lot, but he knew homesickness wasn't the real reason for her tears. He was the cause. Him and that agent in Nashville and the possibility of a future different from the one he'd planned.

An hour ago, he'd realized what he had to do. If Carol's happiness depended upon singing, then that's what he wanted her to do. They might starve to death while she tried to make it in show business, but they would starve together.

Husbands, love your wives, the apostle Paul had written to the Ephesians, *just as Christ loved the church and gave himself up for her.*

Jonathan loved Carol that much. He needed her to know it.

"Was that your folks on the phone?" he asked.

She turned, eyes wide with surprise. "I ... I didn't expect you home yet."

He stepped toward her. "The store will have to close without me tonight."

She gave him an uncertain smile.

"I love you, Carol." He took another step forward.

She drew a shaky breath. "I love you too, Johnny."

His heart caught. Did she mean those words after the silence, disappointment, and hurt? More, did she believe in his love for her?

He took hold of one of her hands and drew her into the living room. "I don't think you should wait for your present until morning. I want you to have it now."

"You do? But—"

"Close your eyes."

"But I—"

"Go on. Close your eyes."

She obeyed his request.

"Keep them shut tight." He led her around to the front of the sofa, then had her sit, guiding her with his hands on her upper arms. He glanced over his shoulder at the new guitar resting next to the tree, a red bow tied around its waist. With a quick prayer that she would like it as much as he wanted her to, he said, "Okay, open them."

If he lived to be a hundred, he would never forget the expression that crossed her face when she saw that guitar.

"Johnny." She rose and stepped toward the instrument, lifting it from its rest before turning to look at him. "Johnny, it's a Martin."

"The guy said it's one of the best. But we can exchange it if you don't like it."

"Of course I like it." She held it close to her body. "I would be crazy not to. But we can't afford it. You've said so yourself."

He shrugged. "I sold a few things. Borrowed a little more. And we'll eat beans if we have to. You need the best if you're going to Nashville."

Her eyes widened. "Nashville?"

"Carol, Travis Thompson and Ken Hill are right. You're amazing. I can't hold you back from something you want this much. Not ever." He moved toward her. "You're more important to me than anything else, and I'll go to Nashville or Timbuktu and find a way to buy you a hundred Martins if that's what'll make you happy."

"Oh, Johnny." A tiny sob caught in her throat. "I don't ... I don't know what to say."

"As long as you love me, Carol, you don't need to say anything more."

She stepped into his open arms. "I do love you, Johnny. I do."

In the wee hours of Christmas morning, Carol sat in the living room of their apartment, the new guitar resting on her thigh, the agent's business card once again in her hand. The lights on the Christmas tree provided the only illumination in the room, but it was enough for her purpose.

A tune played in her mind, one she'd toyed with for the past two weeks. She'd tried to find lyrics to fit the simple melody. Tried and failed.

Take delight in the Lord, the psalmist wrote, *and he will give you the desires of your heart.*

Wasn't the desire of her heart to sing? Hadn't it always been?

She looked at Ken Hill's card again, the black print unreadable in the red and green lights of the tree.

Carol loved music. She loved singing. She loved writing songs. From the time she was a little girl, it had been her dream to perform professionally. Now it could all come true. Everything she'd ever hoped for.

Johnny...

Her husband was willing to give up everything for her. He loved her enough to lay down his whole life, to give up the approval of his father, perhaps his future in the family business, maybe the eventual completion of his college education. And all for her.

She whispered, "You called me to sing, Lord. And now Johnny agrees. Why am I still so unsettled?"

The answer came in an instant, simple and yet profound. *I called you to sing, beloved, but are you willing to sing only for Me?*

The words of the psalmist resounded in her heart: *Take delight in the Lord and he will give you the desires of your heart. Commit your way to the Lord; trust in him and he will do this.*

She understood then, as she hadn't before, what the psalmist was saying. God hadn't promised to give Carol what she wanted because she delighted in Him. God had promised that when she delighted in Him, the desires of her heart would change and be what He wanted for her.

"What's Your desire for my heart, Lord?"

As if in answer to her prayer, that melody played in her mind, but this time she heard the lyrics too. She tossed the business card onto the coffee table, closed her eyes, and began to pluck the guitar strings.

"I want to sing you a carol for Christmas ... One that comes straight from my heart ..."

Yes, she was willing to sing only for the Lord, if that was His plan, and yes, she knew His desire for her now. It was Jonathan. That's why God had brought them together. She'd known it ... and then she'd forgotten it.

"I want to sing you a carol for Christmas ... But I don't know where to start ..."

I'm sorry, Lord. I'm sorry for not listening to You, for striving against You, for wanting my own willful way.

"Carol?"

She looked toward the bedroom doorway where Jonathan stood, clad in pajamas, his hair mussed from sleep. He looked wonderful. Perfect. Her very heart's desire.

"What are you doing up at this hour?" He rubbed his eyes. "If you're waiting for Santa, you should know he already brought your present." He motioned toward the guitar.

"I know." She smiled. "Now he's brought one for you."

He raised an eyebrow in question.

Tomorrow she would tell Jonathan everything God revealed to her this night. Tomorrow she would tell him she wasn't going to Nashville. Tomorrow she would tell him she wouldn't go until God told them both it was His will, *if* He ever said it was His will. But right now, she had other things to tell Jonathan.

She patted the sofa. "Come sit with me."

With a smile of curiosity curving his mouth, he joined her.

She began to sing again, louder this time, repeating the first stanza of the love song the Lord had given her. Then she stopped and met his gaze. "Johnny Burke, you're my heart's desire. I know I haven't shown it the way I should lately, but it's true."

Before he could reply, she began to sing again.

"I want to sing you a carol for Christmas … A melody full of joy from above … I want to sing you a carol for Christmas … Johnny, it's always you I will love."

He didn't move or speak for several moments after she fell silent. Then he grinned, a teasing glint in his eyes. "It probably won't make the Top Twenty, but I like it."

She laughed as she set the guitar aside. "You'd better." Then she snuggled into her husband's waiting embrace, placing her head on his shoulder. "It may be the only present you get this year."

He kissed her hair. "Sweetheart, you're the only present that matters to me. For Christmas or any other time of the year." He pulled her closer. "I'm happy as long as you'll be *my* Carol for Christmas."

Epilogue

Christmas Day, Two Years Later

Carol came awake slowly, reluctantly. She released a soft groan as she opened her eyes. Weak sunlight filtered through the blinds.

"Hey, sleepyhead," Jonathan greeted her. "Merry Christmas."

She turned her head on the pillow. Her husband sat in the chair beside the bed, grinning at her.

"How're you feeling?"

She groaned again, but this time with a smile.

Jonathan leaned forward and kissed her. "You look beautiful. Absolutely radiant."

He was being kind, bless him. She'd been in labor for almost twenty-four hours before giving birth to their daughter at 2:08 this morning. Beautiful was the last thing she must look.

"Good morning." A nurse entered the hospital room, rolling the cart that held their daughter. "Are we ready to nurse the baby?"

"I'm ready." She searched for the control to raise the head of the bed.

After checking to make certain the hospital bands on mother and daughter matched, the nurse brought the baby to her. Little Elena Christine wore a small pink-knitted cap on her head, covering her dark hair, and she was wrapped tightly in a white receiving blanket with pink and blue stripes.

Overwhelming love welled in Carol's heart as she welcomed the infant into her arms. For a moment, her thoughts returned to Christmas two years before. She remembered the moment of revelation when she understood nothing she wanted could ever be as great as what God wanted to give her. He'd changed the desires of her heart, and look who it brought her.

She lifted her eyes from the baby to meet Jonathan's gaze. "I love you, Johnny," she whispered.

He kissed her again, slow and sweet, before kissing the baby's cap-covered head. "And I love you. Both of you. You've made me the happiest guy in the world."

"Isn't she gorgeous?"

"Just like her mother."

Carol smiled.

"You'll have to write her a song."

"Mmm."

Someday, perhaps she would be able to write a song for Elena. For now, the melody in her heart was one of indescribable joy.

Thank You, Father. Thank You for giving me the desires of Your heart.

Coming in July 2007, the continuation of
the Burke family's story

Return to Me
Robin Lee Hatcher

Chapter 1

*T*here exists a strange moment between sleep and
wakefulness when dreams cease and realism
remains at bay. That was when Roxy's heart spoke to her
most clearly.

It's time to go home.

Roxanne Burke had given Nashville seven years to dis-
cover her. She'd offered her voice, her face—and eventually, her body—but despite her best efforts and dedication,
despite her desperate grasps at the brass ring, country music
and stardom didn't want her. Roxy was worse than a has-
been. She was a never-was.

I've gotta go home.

Fully awake now, she covered her face with her hands
as a groan rumbled in her chest. Did she have a home to

return to? When she left Idaho, she'd burned her bridges with a blowtorch. She'd said hateful things to her family when they tried to convince her not to go. She'd been young and foolish and full of herself. So certain she could take on the world. So certain she was meant for greatness. So certain...

Roxy opened her eyes and looked around the studio apartment. The clock said it was almost 6:00 p.m.—depression and hunger had kept her in bed all day—but only anemic light filtered through the miniblinds, making the dismal room look worse than it was. Or maybe the lighting showed the place in stark reality. It was a dump, but it was the best she could afford.

Can almost afford.

She was unemployed and five days late with the rent. She hadn't eaten since yesterday after she pocketed a stale doughnut from the break room at Matthews and Jeffries Talent Agency. Pete Jeffries hadn't represented her in three years—she'd burned that bridge too—but she'd gone crawling to him, hoping for a gig of some kind. Something. Anything. In the end, she hadn't asked. When she saw the pity in his eyes, she couldn't stay. She'd seen herself as he saw her. Pathetic. Dark circles under her eyes. Waif-thin. Limp, lifeless hair. Thrift-store clothes in need of an iron.

Bile rose in her throat, and Roxy bolted from the bed, rushing to the bathroom. She heaved over the toilet, but there was nothing in her stomach to lose. Tears burned her eyes.

Go home.

Roxy's shaky legs wouldn't hold her upright any longer, and she crumpled onto the linoleum, weak and pitiful. Curling into a fetal position on the cool floor, she remembered the words she hurled at her family the day she left Boise.

"Next time you hear from me, my name will be on a CD. You'll see."

Pride was a wretched thing. Pride had kept her from responding to the messages they left on her answering machine. Her boyfriend stopped calling before the first year was out, but not her father and Elena. They persisted. Of course, when she no longer could afford a telephone, she severed that thin lifeline too.

Was everyone healthy? Was her sister married, maybe even a mom by now? Roxy didn't know. No CD, no contact.

Seven years. Seven years of silence. Would they even want to hear from her? Would they want to see her again?

Go home. Find out.

"Oh, God. How can I go back? Look at me."

How had she sunk this low? When her family learned all that she'd done, they would despise her. The men. The booze. And worse...

Roxy had read a novel about ancient Rome a year or so ago. In it, Caesar invited a woman who displeased him to open a vein, meaning she could commit suicide rather than face a worse death. The woman climbed into a tub of hot water and cut her wrists with a sharp knife. The hot water caused her to bleed faster, and death came without pain.

Was that true? Was it painless to end one's life that way? Perhaps Roxy should spare her father the shame of seeing her. She no longer had promise or beauty. She was a washed-out, used-up, discarded nobody.

I'd be better off dead.

Yet even in her miserable state, Roxy didn't want to die. Which was why she would go home, tail tucked between her legs, a capital *L* for *Loser* stamped upon her forehead. She would beg her family's forgiveness and eat whatever crow was required. Better eat crow than go hungry in this stinking hole.

She drew a deep breath, then slowly pushed up onto her hands and knees. Her head dropped forward between her arms. She gulped several times, begging the room not to spin. After it steadied, she sat on her heels. Peeking over the countertop, she caught a glimpse of her reflection in the mirror. Just the top half of her head, but that was more than enough. She groaned again.

Where was she going to get the money for bus fare? She'd lost her last job and no one would hire her looking like this. The friends she had when flush with her grandmother's inheritance had long since disappeared. So had the handsome, ambitious men who used to squire her to parties and premiers.

Pete Jeffries was her only hope. Pete, with the pity in his eyes. She would have to go back to see him. She would have to beg his help before she could beg her father's forgiveness.

Maybe Caesar's open-vein solution was the better option.

This was the night. Elena Burke felt it in her bones. This was the night Wyatt Baldini would propose.

She stared at her reflection in the floor-length mirror. A diamond-and-gold choker. Teardrop earrings. A simple but elegant black dress that ended an inch above her knees. Red toe nails and killer heels with slinky straps around her ankles.

When a woman gets engaged, she should look like a million. Elena was no great beauty, but she came close to it tonight.

Someone rapped on her outer office door, then she heard it open.

"Just a minute," she called.

"It's me, Elena. May I come in?"

She stepped out of the bathroom that adjoined her office. "Of course, Dad."

Jonathan Burke let out a low whistle when he saw her. "Well, look at you."

"Wyatt and I are going to dinner. He's supposed to pick me up in about fifteen minutes." She closed the distance between them, leaning forward to kiss her father on the cheek. "What about you? What are you doing tonight?"

"A quiet evening at home for me."

Elena's father was a distinguished-looking man. In his late fifties, he still had a full head of hair, although it was now steel-gray instead of the dark brown it had been in his youth. His hazel eyes revealed intelligence and an enthusiasm for life that many half his age didn't enjoy.

Her father cocked an eyebrow. "Does Wyatt realize how lucky he is to have someone special like you?"

She felt herself flush.

"About time." He touched her cheek with his fingertips. "It's good to see you happy, honey."

Elena loved her father. There wasn't much she wouldn't do for him. Elena had enjoyed a special bond with her father and had wanted to grow up to be just like him. With that goal in mind, she attended college, got her degree, and immediately went to work in the corporate offices of Burke Department Stores. She supposed it was in her blood.

Her great-grandfather, Dillon Burke, had opened a small clothing store on Tenth Street back in the thirties, before the start of World War II. With hard work and smart decisions, Dillon and his son Arlen built that shop into an upscale department-store chain. Then her father had multiplied the successes of his grandfather and father. Now there were Burke Department Stores in twenty-five states, and Elena was a vice president in the family firm, her father's right-hand gal.

"Wyatt's a fine man," Jonathan said, pulling her thoughts to the present. "I'll be glad to call him my son-in-law."

Her father had spoken similar words many years ago. But not to Elena.

A shudder moved up her spine.

"You okay, honey?"

She forced a smile. "I'm fine, Dad." Glancing at her watch, she added, "But I'd better finish getting ready. Wyatt will be here soon."

Roxy crawled back into bed, shivering as she lay between the threadbare sheets that were rough and wrinkled against her skin.

"I'm hungry," she whispered. But she might as well try to eat those words, because her wallet was as empty as her belly.

When was the last time she had a decent meal? Too long ago to remember.

She thought of the homeless people she'd seen going through garbage receptacles behind restaurants. Once she'd felt nothing for the homeless but disgust. Why didn't they simply get jobs and stop being an eyesore to society? Now it frightened her to think of them, to think how close to being one of them she was. Perhaps what frightened her more was the temptation to go search behind restaurants for food.

I won't be hungry when I get home.

She closed her eyes and imagined the house where she grew up. Five bedrooms. A large game room. Vaulted ceilings. Maids' quarters. A spacious kitchen filled with all the modern conveniences. Family. A home filled with love.

It seemed long ago and far away. Had she ever lived in such a place? Had she ever been unconditionally loved? Was it all a dream?

Tears slipped from behind her eyelids and dampened the pillow under her head.

God, help me get home.

The slender candle in the center of the table had burned low. The fine china and crystal had been cleared and the white tablecloth swept clean of crumbs. Music—a familiar love song—wafted toward them from the baby grand at the opposite side of the restaurant.

Wyatt leaned toward Elena. "You look beautiful tonight."

She might have returned the compliment. Wyatt was the sort of man who caused women's heads to turn no matter where he was. Whether clad in a suit, as he was tonight, or in jeans and a T-shirt, his Mediterranean good looks—black hair, deep blue eyes, dark complexion—made him stand out in a crowd.

"Did I already tell you that?" he asked.

"Yes." She smiled. "But I don't mind you saying it again."

Of course she didn't mind. While Elena loved Wyatt with all her heart and had for a long, long time, she wasn't blind to his shortcomings, one of those being that he wasn't generous with compliments. Perhaps that was because he didn't require the praise and reassurances of others, so he didn't think others needed them either.

"There's something important I need to tell you," Wyatt said after a brief silence.

They had spoken of many things during the course of the evening—his work, her work, his mother, her father, the Sunday school class he taught, the women's Bible study she led—but there'd been no mention of a future together.

Elena fought hard to keep her disappointment in check. She'd been certain this was the night he would—

"I'm leaving my law practice, Elena."

Her eyes widened. "You're what?"

"I'm leaving it. I've decided to enter seminary."

"Seminary?" So that was what had been on his mind in recent weeks. It hadn't been thoughts of her after all.

"I've felt God calling me into full-time ministry for some time now, but I wanted to wait for confirmation before I told you."

Elena pasted on another smile. "You'll make a wonderful pastor, Wyatt. I'm happy for you." Truly, she was. Their shared faith in Christ was important to her. That God would call Wyatt into the ministry didn't surprise her. Not really. It was just—

"There's only one thing I'm not sure of." He reached a hand across the table to take hold of hers, and she felt his gaze looking beyond her eyes and into her heart. "Would you ever consider becoming a pastor's wife?"

Her breath caught in her throat. Strange, earlier this evening she'd expected his proposal, but now that it had come, it took her by surprise.

"I love you, Elena. Will you marry me?"

She blinked away tears of joy. "Yes, Wyatt. Yes, I'll marry you."